MW00450682

"*The Winning Link* takes people on the business success journey by sharing the strategic objective, clarifying expectations, measuring performance, and then having meaningful conversations about how any performance gaps can be addressed. He engages with people through a consistent process that enables them to perform to their best—which creates confidence, goodwill, and a winning formula for all."

—Malcolm McDowell
Chief Executive Officer, Note Printing Australia Limited,
A subsidiary of the Reserve Bank of Australia

"When Billy assumed responsibility for my operation, my wife asked, 'Isn't it going to be difficult working for one of your best friends?' I responded, 'not at all, I just gained the best employee I will ever have.' Billy is the definition of a resonant leader. As a friend, a peer, and a former member of Billy's staff, I've been a witness to the *The Winning Link* firsthand for close to 20 years. It enables what many leaders fail to achieve, empowerment."

—Ellis Jones
VP & Chief Sustainability Officer Goodyear Tire & Rubber Co.

"*The Winning Link* engages every employee—plant leader to operators—to work on the common purpose to be great. Through mutual respect, setting clear expectations, visible performance tracking, and closed loop accountability, predictable improvement results consistently follow."

—D. Keith Hamilton
Vice President Operations Georgia-Pacific LLC

"Billy Taylor is one of my most trusted business advisors. He has helped me create a culture of ownership and accountability that has propelled our growth while creating a workplace where our people are empowered to do their best work."

—Jeffrey Scott Jones
Founder & CEO Consolidus, LLC, 5X Inc. 5000 Fastest
Growing Business, according to *Inc. Magazine*

"Billy Taylor's engaging approach to operational alignment by building clarity of ownership, alignment of objectives, and collaboration toward strategic vision through storytelling and easy mnemonic devices make the process improvement journey fun and unthreatening at every level of the organization. As the team moves from 'No' to 'Know' their areas by defining what is winning and creating clear pathways to achieve its CPI's by tracking KPA's and KPI's, the level of purposeful engagement on the floor increases. My favorite part of the process is how simple it is to implement - you don't need a doctorate in business to adopt Billy's approach, just commitment to communicating differently to ensure the strategy is not a secret and then giving operators control of their results through clarity. Billy has helped our team simplify the engagement process and accelerate our journey toward excellence."

—Ryan Plotkin
President, MD Building Products

"Understanding the delicate balance between people and process gives Billy an edge that most leaders struggle to maintain. *The Winning Link* is an extremely insightful roadmap to assist business leaders in developing and maintaining this balance in their own operations. When the balance is met, the whole company wins."

—Jessica Sublett, JD, LLM
Chief Operating Officer, Bounce Innovation

"Billy excels at building a cohesive team, aligning them around a clearly defined target, creating processes that lead to 'winning' and making the score visible and obvious. I still use his clarifying concept featured in *The Winning Link* of 'Define, Align and Execute' in strategy planning, in operating reviews and in my daily conversations with my leadership team."

—Bart Reimer
Vice President of Operations, Charter Steel

"*The Winning Link* is a hallmark of how to be a highly successful manager. I first encountered Billy Taylor on the campus of Prairie View A&M. I was there to interview management candidates. My initial impression has proven true for 30-plus years. This book features his strategy for leadership, executive charisma, organizational skills, and business and emotional intelligence from his career leading a Fortune 500 North America Operations. *The Winning Link* is an outstanding work of art. Congratulations, Billy T., and thank you for sharing."

—Greg Guy
Goodyear Tire & Rubber Company

THE
WINNING
LINK

THE WINNING LINK

A Proven Process to Define, Align, and Execute Strategy at Every Level

BILLY RAY TAYLOR

New York   Chicago   San Francisco   Athens   London   Madrid
Mexico City   Milan   New Delhi   Singapore   Sydney   Toronto

1 2 3 4 5 6 7 8 9 LCR   27 26 25 24 23 22

ISBN: 978-1-264-26826-9
MHID: 1-264-26826-2

e-ISBN: 978-1-264-26827-6
e-MHID: 1-264-26827-0

McGraw Hill books are available at special quantity discounts to use as premiums and sales promotions or for use in corporate training programs. To contact a representative, please visit the Contact Us pages at www.mhprofessional.com.

McGraw Hill is committed to making our products accessible to all learners. To learn more about the available support and accommodations we offer, please contact us at accessibility@mheducation.com. We also participate in the Access Text Network (www.accesstext.org), and ATN members may submit requests through ATN.

I am dedicating this book to my guardian angel, Fleater Dawson King. First and foremost, praises and thanks to God, the Almighty, for blessing me with her to guide me in life. She was, and continues to be, my guiding light. Many of the examples and quotes I reference in this book come from her teachings during my upbringing. She was my legal guardian. She instilled in me the core values of respect for people, establishing and holding to personal standards, and the commitment to hard work. She also believed, that to make life easy, keep it simple.

In her final days here on earth, she asked me a profound question, "When a bird lands on a branch does it trust the branch, or does it trust its wings?" Before I could answer, she stated, "I have seen many birds land on branches son, but what I have never seen, is that branch break and the bird fall and die! Trust your wings in your journey through life, and you will be rewarded with success."

Trusting the process is what I have done throughout my career, which has been a rewarding experience. Building trust with my employees, in the process and the assets we manage, is a principle imbedded in the LinkedXL process. You were right, dear "Aunt Fleater," I still and will continue to trust my wings. May you rest in peace. Thank you for eternally investing in me.

CONTENTS

FOREWORD

Billy Taylor has tremendous insight into how organizations can reach their goals and fulfill their purpose. I'm very glad this book will give a broader audience the opportunity to learn from his talent and experience.

I met Billy at a pivotal time for my own organization, as head of operations for Note Printing Australia, which prints Australia's banknotes and passports. In 1988, Australia issued the world's first polymer banknote. Australia invented polymer banknote technology, and it's a point of national pride.

Today, there are more than 75 billion polymer banknotes in circulation. In the last 30 years, more than 30 countries have issued in excess of 175 denominations on polymer. During the early 1990s, the Reserve Bank of Australia converted all Australia's notes to polymer. The technology served us well, with very low counterfeiting rates for more than 25 years.

When we aren't printing banknotes for Australia, we print them for other countries, mostly in the Asia Pacific area. Material and labor costs are very high and quality is crucial. After all, money is a nation's business card.

In the late 2000's, Australia revised its banknote series with additional security features and technologies to keep a step ahead of counterfeiters. We had to upgrade our manufacturing and printing line, replacing all printing presses and adding higher-level security features to both our design process and our printing capabilities.

This represented a paradigm shift in security printing for some of the printers who worked for us. They'd come up making mechanical adjustments to presses by hand, and now it was all computers and servo-controls. Some workers retired to let the next generation take the reins. Between our need to install and commission all the new equipment, retrain the existing printing staff, train new printing staff, design and build a more complex banknote that's harder to counterfeit, and run what seemed to be a never-ending series of development trials, we had our hands full. We made a deliberate decision to pull out of the export market long enough to finish the transition to the upgraded banknote series. Our priority is delivering what the Reserve Bank of Australia needs.

Creating the new banknote series would take up all our capacity. Once the new banknotes were launched and in circulation, however, we would print only enough money to replace unfit notes, so we would have excess capacity.

We knew that we needed to get back into the global exports market if we were to keep the people we'd spent a lot of time developing. That meant developing the export business while the currency launch was still underway, without affecting the orders we had committed to the Reserve Bank of Australia.

That's when I met Billy at a workshop run by Michael Bremer for the Association for Manufacturing Excellence (AME Australia). I knew instantly in listening to Billy that he had some profound knowhow and wisdom. After several conversations that day, we agreed to meet for dinner. That evening Billy offered me deeper insights and glimpses of his system: lightbulbs flashed. I realized quickly that this man is gold. Our CEO kept saying, "We need to be a measured organization." I thought we were well measured, but I didn't really understand what he meant by that until I met Billy. When I saw Billy's process, I realized that this system and process was exactly what we needed, and what our CEO was calling for without being able to articulate it. This was the missing link for us, and I daresay for many organizations.

Billy and I kept in touch and I found the ongoing dialog very insightful. I think he got sick of me continually following up with more questions; he invited me to spend a week at the Goodyear plant in Akron, Ohio, that Billy managed under his North America Tire footprint. Between Billy and his leadership team, I saw all parts of the process. It was a deep immersion in a mature excellence system, and the best week of my life for learning and development. I'm still boggled by Billy's generosity in spending so much time with me.

The 2019 Australian AME conference brought Billy back to Australia for a keynote address. He also did a week of consulting for Note Printing Australia, helping to boost our improvement journey to another level. Billy helped us define winning and put the infrastructure in place to track, measure, and cascade our key performance actions. Using this method, our people see how their work is connected to the overall strategy. They can ask for help as they need it, instead of existing in pockets of isolation or (worse) "hiding in the herd."

Billy's system has helped us identify the blockages we needed to address to put us on a path to stability, developing overseas relationships and filling our excess capacity with exports work as we settle the second Australian polymer series into its replenishment phase. We were developing our overseas market long before we thought possible, delivering on our strategy. We have put the relationships in place and are moving forward, capitalizing on the freed capacity, and making the best use of our assets and (most importantly) our people.

A generous, open, and caring man, Billy is the personification of a servant leader. He is a brilliant storyteller—after 10 minutes interviewing Billy, a top speaking coach said that she had "nothing to teach him!" It's no surprise that he can fully hold the attention of 2,500 people as a keynote speaker. He makes the complex simple, brings out the best in people, and gives much more than he takes. He has left a trail of very grateful managers and leaders, all aspiring to be the best version of themselves.

I'm excited that, through this book, *The Winning Link*, Billy is reaching an even broader audience. I think you'll find him every bit as insightful as I have.

Peter Ballas
Note Printing Australia
January 2022

THE
WINNING
LINK

CHAPTER 1

Defining Winning

With its long history of racism, the Deep South isn't a logical destination for a young African American man. I still moved to Fayetteville, North Carolina, in 2010. The CEO of Goodyear had assigned me to lead a complete transformation for a large-scale manufacturing plant with a budget of $372 million and 3,100 unionized employees. The task was to develop and implement an effective, sustainable operating system and structure that let the plant be a reliable, low-cost supplier. The first step was to go and see the reality of the plant. Did the enterprise know what winning meant? Did it have a strategy to achieve its goals, or was hope the only strategy?

At all of 38 years old, I was head of a failing tire factory. It should have been producing a total of 38,000 tires a day for automobile manufacturers and retail tire stores across America. Instead, it only made between 30,000 and 31,000 tires a day. To compound the issue, it was also making the wrong tires. The running joke at that plant was that, to hit the number, tires needed to be nothing more than "round and black and out the back."

I arguably had the background that I needed to put the Fayetteville plant to rights. After graduating from Prairie View A&M, I started with The Goodyear Tire & Rubber Co. in June 1989. I was a management trainee in Freeport, Illinois, and my first assignment was as a third-shift floor manager. Goodyear initially trained me in a management philosophy called Theory X, then transitioned me to another called Theory Y. My first 12 years at Goodyear were in a unionized labor environment.

It was in Freeport, Illinois, in 1997 that I met one of my most important mentors: Larry Robbins, a force to be reckoned with who set a nonnegotiably high standard. He was the role model and coach I needed, the first person who took me under his wing and mentored me. Larry demonstrated the importance of setting and living by standards. He didn't play favorites. In the Freeport plant, Larry's rules applied to everyone under his leadership—including Larry.

I advanced through a series of positions at Goodyear. I spent 12 years in Freeport. Then I was promoted to plant manager in Kingman, Arizona, where the factory wasn't unionized. In 2001, I was the first black person to work at the facility. The plant taught me the value of extreme ownership and autonomous work teams. In two years under my leadership, the plant broke every record for safety, quality, productivity, and output in its 20-year history. To accomplish this, I used what I would come to call lean operational excellence. I'd read about the lean manufacturing philosophy in books such as *The Goal* and *The Toyota Way*. I'd had no formal training in it.

After the success in Kingman, Larry recommended I take a step back from my job as plant manager to become Goodyear's business center manager in Topeka, Kansas. Larry felt that I needed more development in leading others and managing processes.

Not incidentally, Larry had been promoted from production manager to plant manager in Topeka. It was there that I learned about authentic continuous improvement and lean manufacturing. I also learned how to partner with the union. Under Larry, we again broke every quality, safety, productivity, output, and revenue performance record in the department's history. The key to success was how we effectively executed strategy and built cultural norms on how we win, work, and align on our focal points.

Personal and professional growth were part of the learning and development Larry envisioned for me when he sent me to Tyler, Texas, when he thought I was ready to lead change in a more hostile environment. Larry told me about the challenges of a plant in the Deep South for a black person, but he emphasized that change is not about black and white. It's about culture and how culture controls strategy. I was the plant's first African American plant manager.

In Tyler we leveraged what we knew about how to win within a union environment, delivering milestone performance in key indicators. From Tyler, I was promoted to Lawton, Oklahoma, Goodyear's flagship plant. Again, there were no minorities on the plant's senior leadership team in Lawton. After setting new plant performance milestones and winning the Shingo Silver Medalion— the Nobel prize of manufacturing—I was expecting to be promoted to director of manufacturing for North America. Instead I was assigned to Fayetteville, North Carolina, another underperforming plant. My mission was to take Fayetteville from losing to winning.

It may not be apparent from this narrative, but each time I took on a new leadership challenge, I was scared to death. Where would I start? Why would they follow me? In this book I share with you the principles and methods

I learned throughout this journey and give you a direct look at how I have applied these in my work at Goodyear, especially in turning around the Fayetteville plant.

WHAT DOES "WINNING" MEAN?

If you're reading this book, you might also have an organization you'd like to take from losing to winning. Or maybe your company is doing well enough, but you'd like to move it from "pretty good" to "truly excellent."

In the ecosystem of business, success rests on the mutual dependence of people, processes, and assets. This book will function as a GPS system to guide you to business success, focusing on the personal and interpersonal aspects of leading a winning company. In it, I describe how organizations can effectively define, align, and execute strategies for growth and profitability.

This book is called *The Winning Link*, and in it, I talk a lot about winning. Obviously, there are many ways to define "winning," from scoring more points than the other team to enjoying dominance in the court of public opinion. When I talk about winning, I mean deliberate success. Plenty of businesses wander, bumble, or even stagger into a state of affairs where things are pretty good. The organization is making money, at least some of the time. It's able to pay its employees and hang onto many of its clients.

That's not what I want for the organizations I manage, or for the people who read this book. I want you to succeed on purpose.

> My organizations and yours deserve nothing less than defined goals achieved in strategic ways.

My organizations and yours deserve nothing less than defined goals achieved in strategic ways.

The LinkedXL operating process, which builds on Toyota's lean manufacturing principles, gives you a system that works to help you set goals, determine strategies to meet those goals, and assign ownership to execute the strategies. This book will teach you to connect strategy and goals to individual contributions and get your people to own their responsibilities. *The Winning Link* gives you a visual management system so that you can tell, in 10 seconds or less, what's going right (or wrong) in your company. It takes a scientific approach to improvement and helps you embed the system in your company culture so that it outlasts your time there.

You will never again stumble around in the dark, hoping that you're doing and driving the right things. You won't need to wonder if what you're doing is good enough, or whether you're making progress. Winning means driving your organization to success with all the lights on.

MAKE YOUR GOAL EXTREMELY CLEAR

In theory, organizations understand how to set goals, develop a strategy for reaching those goals, and create an execution plan for that strategy. You might think that you're out of the dark at that point. In practicality, things aren't quite that simple. You won't execute winning without extreme clarity and extreme ownership.

When I left Tyler to become plant manager of the Goodyear factory in Fayetteville, North Carolina, I knew that the factory needed to make 38,000 specification-compliant, high-quality tires every day. The finance controller, supply chain manager, and outgoing plant manager knew it, too. But the thousands of people who worked at that plant didn't know.

I needed everyone in the Fayetteville Goodyear plant to understand that winning meant making 38,000 high-quality tires that met specifications for each order. But I didn't want to be the person who told crowds of workers this over and over again, drumming it into their heads until they tuned me out from boredom and annoyance.

So I ordered a bright yellow football jersey for every employee in the plant. The number on the front of the jersey was 38, for the 38,000 tires we needed to make every day (Figure 1.1). The back of the jersey featured the word "choice," because we wanted the Fayetteville Goodyear facility to be every customer's top choice. One sleeve displayed the winged foot that is Goodyear's logo; the other sleeve sported the union emblem.

FIGURE 1.1 Original 38 Team Jersey

Every employee got a jersey, a letter thanking them for being part of the Goodyear team, and a newsletter, all sent to their homes. The newsletter explained the jersey and announced that we would clean up the plant and host a family day. Our goal was not only to engage the employees, but also to establish a sense of pride in the jobs they did and where they did it. We invited employees to wear their jerseys and bring their families to see the place they worked.

That "38" got tons of airplay. When it arrived at employees' homes, workers of course saw it. Their families saw it, too, and asked, "Why is there a big 38 on the shirt?" Then the jerseys left home. People wore that shirt all over Fayetteville, in restaurants, churches, drugstores, and just walking down the street. Everywhere the jersey went, people asked the same question: "Why is the number 38 on the front of the shirt?"

Employees who wore the shirts answered that question all day long. But the question went with the shirt, even if employees gave the shirt away. The shirt is now a collector's item, still inspiring the question about the number.

By widely dispersing an item that had the right question and answer embedded in it, we made the goal of 38,000 tires a day go viral. By the end of that month, at least half of Fayetteville knew that the Goodyear plant needed to make 38,000 tires every day. I didn't have to worry about whether the news would reach every employee. An employee would have needed to leave the country or spend that month unconscious to avoid learning that winning meant making 38,000 tires a day.

We accomplished that by focusing on strategic, practical messaging, both formal and informal. We zeroed in on four components of deliberate clarity:

- **Clarity.** Our message was clear and concise. It was couched in language that our target audience readily understood. It outlined our expectation and issued a call to action.
- **Specificity.** The information was sufficiently targeted to get an exact message across, but not overexplained or condescending.
- **Relevancy.** It's hard to get more relevant than the goal your employer needs to achieve in order to stay in business.
- **Delivery.** The plant's financial controller wasn't thrilled about the $15,000 I spent on the shirts. But they did a fantastic job of spreading our message. We also used strategically placed TV monitors, social media content, and town hall meetings.

ADMIT THE NEED FOR CHANGE

The evolution of excellence begins with admitting the need for change. To solve any problem, you must first admit to yourself that the problem exists. This isn't necessarily an easy thing to do. You've probably put a lot of effort into your professional life, and you care about the things that you do. I doubt you want to think of yourself (for instance) as a substandard worker or a less-than-adequate parent.

If the failing isn't solely your own, an understanding of just how much work would be involved in fixing the problem can prevent you from admitting that there is an issue. When the sports team you own loses a game, for instance, it's much more convenient to tell yourself that they just had a bad day than it is to consider completely overhauling coaching and management.

In other situations, you might understand that things aren't right, but find it difficult and confusing to put your finger precisely on the problem. This book will help you determine where things are going off the rails in your organization as well as uncover ways that cause it to fall short of its goals. But the diagnosis is a process, and executives first need to be brave enough to commit to change and begin that exploration.

Other leaders ignore problems because they fear a loss of popularity. It's much more pleasant to be the bearer of good news than of bad. Leaders must learn to choose being respected over being liked. Leaders should treat other people with fairness and respect, but it's not their job to try to please everyone or to avoid disagreement at all costs. Open discussion and debate fuels creativity, collaboration, confirmation, and conviction. As a leader, you need to be comfortable with discomfort, as well as having uncomfortable (but necessary) conversations.

Whatever the reason, it often seems easier and nicer to kid ourselves than to face up to reality. Plenty of people simply stop here, minimizing and avoiding the issues that plague their organizations.

DELIBERATE CLARITY: MANAGING THE UGLY BABY

Once you're brave enough to admit the problem to yourself, you have the task of bringing other people to a point of similar honesty. Here you will meet what I call ugly baby syndrome.

Imagine that your friend has a new baby. "Isn't he beautiful?" your friend asks when you visit. Because you are smart, you realize that this is not a real question. Babies (and brides) are beautiful by definition. In reality, many newborn babies are kind of funny looking. Their heads are malleable. They've just been squeezed through a tight exit, and they're not yet acclimated to life in the outside world. They shriek; they poop in their pants.

Of course, most babies also have parents who would die to protect them. Tell your friend the truth about the new baby's looks and you risk seriously hurting the new parent's feelings, as well as summoning their protective instincts. Your relationship would take a hit. It might not recover.

In business, an ugly baby is a hard truth. Admitting it involves the discomfort and inconvenience of telling ourselves and others that our best efforts haven't yielded the desired results. That feels a lot like failure. Just thinking about it bruises our egos. Saying it out loud really hurts.

Babies get better looking on their own—they just need a little time. In business, however, converting an ugly baby to a pretty one needs more than just time; it requires a changed mindset. In a corporate setting, you'll need a leader, teams, and individuals who are comfortable talking transparently about and addressing situations in which a truthful response creates stress.

Without honest, straightforward communication with key stakeholders—management, workers, customers, and stock owners—performance and company culture both suffer. Transparency is critically important to any organization because it builds individual and organizational trust and makes employees feel that they are working for a company or leader that has high ethical standards and fosters those standards in others.

We can all tell when an individual or organization's party line is out of step with the facts. Let's pretend for a moment that my doctor says that losing 50 pounds would greatly improve my health. You can say that I'm big-boned, muscular, or athletic, but everyone knows that you're putting a gentler, more positive spin on the truth. The same is true of that ugly baby. You can say that the child has her mother's eyes or her father's chin. But in reality, a baby whose head is a little misshapen from her recent arrival in the world and who has turned magenta from crying isn't all that attractive. You know it; I know it. Even the baby's parents know it.

It's fine to soft-pedal the question of whether a friend is too fat or a baby is ugly, of course. Kindness and social standards almost always require it. When business leaders shade the truth, however, the effort doesn't come off as kind. It's dishonest, and it fosters lack of accountability in the organization's culture.

Transparent leaders and organizations shape enterprise culture. There's a good reason that politicians strive to offer "real talk": Human beings are hardwired to follow leaders we perceive as open and honest. This benefits a business in two ways. First, truthful leaders empower workers to be similarly transparent, bringing facts to the surface that would otherwise stand in the way of executing strategy. Second, truthfulness engages employees, shifting them toward commitment and alignment with a leader's vision.

Telling the truth even when the truth is uncomfortable brings significant benefits. Honesty is the core of every healthy relationship, whether it's a friendship, romance, partnership, or connection between colleagues. An organization can't succeed without building an internal web of honesty and trust.

I want to be specific in explaining what kind of honesty and trust I'm talking about. I'm not saying that you need to share confidential or personal information; leaders can and should have private lives. Necessary transparency means sharing the truths that others need to know to do their jobs well.

In this sense, you're not hurting other people when you talk about the ugly baby. It isn't a service to withhold information, letting stakeholders believe that everything is fine when you see significant problems in a situation. The workers you're leading are presumably intelligent, skilled adults. They deserve the truth and an opportunity to help fix the problems. That's far preferable to hearing nonsense, followed by losing their jobs because a plant closes or an employer goes out of business.

It's also important to be a person who can hear the truth. You need to know about what's happening in other parts of the company. Be careful not to punish people who are brave enough to tell you the truth about what they see going on. The news might not be what you want to hear. Accept it anyway. Think instead of it as a report about symptoms, a necessary part of developing a diagnosis.

Tell the truth and accept the truth, and you'll see greater trust and two-way communication through your organization. Engagement and enterprise advocacy—working for the larger good—will spread as employees work toward a common goal. Your company will benefit from better overall employee motivation as workers confidently take truth-based action.

Note, however, that human beings are not perfectly rational, and complete transparency doesn't rule out bad behavior on the part of leaders, teams, or individual workers. Openness mixed with hidden agendas and manipulation will create a work environment in which workers feel that their autonomy and personality are challenged or attacked. They will (justifiably) retreat or rebel, which is counterproductive to executing any strategy designed to move the company forward. That's why transparency starts with you, and with your understanding of why it's the first necessary element of winning.

Leaders who dodge the ugly baby problem often hope that a problem will go away if they ignore it long enough. Maybe the issue will even solve itself. Sometimes that happens. More often, though the issue becomes a dead fish, stinking up the place and gradually permeating everything it gets near.

YOU CAN'T MANAGE A SECRET

You need to be deliberately clear about the problems you see at your company. You also need to be deliberately clear about how you plan to address those problems.

Organizations fail due to a lack of strategic clarity or because executives arrive at strategic clarity, but don't break it down and transparently tell the rest of the organization. No one can manage a secret. For tactical execution to happen, your plan needs to be clear.

Everyone in your company needs to know about it. Each employee must understand what part of that strategy she owns, as well as how her contribution affects the organization's overall goals.

In many companies, this goes wrong in a variety of ways: leadership that isn't clear about its own goals for the organization or the strategy it will use to meet those goals; a failure to communicate defined goals to everyone in the business; a disconnect between what individuals do every day and the tasks for achieving defined goals; situations where workers don't have what they need to contribute toward reaching goals.

> **No one can manage a secret.**

Some organizations aren't clear on what they're trying to accomplish, so how will they know whether they have or haven't reached their goals? Without clearly defined goals and a way to know that you've reached them (or not), success is a matter of politics, perception, or maybe just the way the boss feels today. Corporate America is full of poorly defined goals, with people being praised or punished for someone's equally vague idea of how well they did or didn't meet those nebulous objectives. It's barely one step better than arbitrary.

Other companies have goals, but haven't clearly defined how they plan to achieve them. They hope to get from an island to the shore but aren't sure if they plan to get there by boat, airplane, swimming, or walking—after they wait for winter to come and the water to freeze over. If you don't know what you want your people to do, how will they figure it out? You must be deliberately clear about your strategy and get into the details. If your team should get to shore by boat, should that boat be a canoe? A motorboat? A dinghy? A yacht? Will they be using sails, oars, or a motor? Are they setting off in January or May?

In still other organizations, the executives know the goals and the strategy for reaching them, but the news hasn't yet reached the masses. Rank-and-file employees have no idea what the company's overall aim is or how it plans to get there. I've been to many meetings in which the C-suite tells me what they hope to achieve, and how they hope to achieve it. But when I pull a random person off the shop floor and ask him to tell me what he knows about the goal and strategy, the inevitable answer is "Not much."

If everyone knows the goals and the strategy to attain them, do all the employees also understand how their individual efforts contribute to the outcome? Imagine that you and four of your friends decide to run a marathon as a group. The organizers explain that they will total the times that each member of the group posts, and the group with the lowest total wins the group competition. In that situation, you can clearly see how your effort contributes to the group's success. You can base your actions—to train well and run at a fast pace—on your knowledge of that contribution. Is the line between each individual's effort and the overall organizational goal that clear for your team members?

Last, but not least, your organization also needs to know how it will be able to tell if it's making progress toward its goals. When you attend a basketball game, everyone there knows that success means scoring more points than the other team. There are set rules and strategies about how the basketball players can score points. At any given moment during the game, you have only to look at the scoreboard to find out how the team is doing. When the game ends—which happens after a specific, rule-governed amount of time—the team with the most points win. "Score more points than the other team" is the one and only goal of every basketball team in the world, but your organization will have its own method of measuring success over time.

EARNING THE RIGHT TO CHANGE

You've revealed the ugly babies and established that your organization needs to change. You know that you need to communicate that to your team, including the strategy and measurable action to get there. Before you can lead the change, however, you'll have to earn the right to change your organization. There are two rights to change: the technical right and the cultural right. Both are necessary to transform an organization and to achieve its goals. Each kind of right also applies to both kinds of change, as I've mapped out in the Table 1.1.

> There are two rights to change: the technical right and the cultural right.

If you're in charge of a company, you already have the technical right to change. The *technical right to change* is asset based. Companies and those who lead them have the technical right to change through their investments in equipment, tools, and employee benefits and compensation. In other words, leaders think they can change things because they own the place. Technically, that's true.

TABLE 1.1 Technical and Cultural Rights to Change

	TECHNICAL CHANGE	CULTURAL CHANGE
TECHNICAL RIGHT TO CHANGE	**Technical right to create technical change** If you have the money and standing as the factory owner, you can buy new equipment.	**Technical right to create cultural change** The leaders have the right to communicate throughout the organization what equipment will be installed and why.
CULTURAL RIGHT TO CHANGE	**Cultural right to create technical change** People need to be well informed and feel confident about new equipment or management structures before you can affect technical change.	**Cultural right to create cultural change** People need to feel that they own a piece of the organization and they are involved in the processes that will use the equipment. Only then will you be able to achieve your goals.

In exchange for the investments, leaders expect certain changes for the better: increased efficiency, lower costs, innovative products and processes, and enhanced company value. But the technical right to change isn't enough by itself. Company cultures don't change just because the people in charge tell them to change, no matter how badly the powers that be want that shift or how much good the adjustment might yield.

To successfully push your organization through change, you will also need to earn the *cultural right to change*. The cultural right to change is about winning hearts and minds. People need to trust their leader and have confidence in the plan for winning. Human beings change most successfully when change happens *with* them, not *to* them.

On a practical level, there are more employees than there are leaders, and leaders can't be everywhere. To win, you need your organization's people to genuinely get behind your plan, not just offer lip service because you control their paychecks.

If companies and leaders don't earn the right to create change, their ability to transform to operational excellence is doomed from the start. Organizations that succeed in executing change and transformation almost always begin that process by establishing *both* the technical and the cultural right to change.

> **Human beings change most successfully when change happens *with* them, not *to* them.**

But as I told *Industry Week* magazine in 2016, most people focus solely on the technical right to change. They don't give enough attention to the cultural right to change, which begins with leaders modeling the way.* Management can't just introduce new tools, processes, and assets and expect positive change to result. Forcing new methods on an unwilling workforce isn't easy or productive; it can even backfire on you. To earn the right to change, organizations and leaders must articulate the case for change persuasively and transparently. That type of people-driven operational excellence flips the organizational chart upside down and puts the company directly in the hands of the workers.

BUILD A CULTURE OF TRANSPARENCY

You win hearts and minds through a long-term commitment to strategic leadership. As a leader, you must

---

* Ginger Christ, "Goodyear's Billy Taylor on Earning the Right to Play the Leadership Game," *IndustryWeek*, May 9, 2016.

develop and articulate an intentionally clear, well-developed, focused critical performance goal and a strategy to get your organization to that goal. Your goal and strategy need to be relevant and believable. You also need to be believable, a transparent leader who does what you say you'll do, especially in supporting the organization's journey to winning.

To use transparency as a leadership tool, you must openly embrace and confront reality, consistently updating the entire company on the state of play. What are your goals? What strategies are you using to reach those goals? What are the challenges facing those strategies? Finally, how is it going? Is the organization on track to meet its goals?

In some companies, the reason that no one communicates the overall strategy and goals is that the C-suite executives haven't actually developed a coherent strategy and goals. I have been in meetings where I have asked each executive to write the company's goals and strategies anonymously on a piece of paper, and then read out the resulting disjointed mess to reinforce this point.

In many instances, top leadership believes wholeheartedly that they have worked out goals and a plan for reaching them. And in reality, they do have a great plan. But they've failed to effectively deploy that strategy by evangelizing to the people who need to know about that plan to support and enact it. Goodyear's top management had goals for the company as a whole and for the factory I was deployed to specifically. But management in that plant had been doing a lousy job of communicating its strategy and goals to the entire organization. Instead, it effectively kept the objectives and strategy secret—and you cannot manage a secret.

The plant especially kept its priorities secret from the people who made the tires. Way up in the air-conditioned corner suites, people in nice suits had gone to a lot of trouble to work out goals and strategies to help the company meet those goals. But down on the shop floor where workers actually made tires, no one knew about those goals and strategies. Those employees were completely in the dark. The manager wanted to win. The workers wanted to win, too. But unless the manager was more effective in sharing the plan with employees, the strategy wouldn't help anyone win.

For transparency to help a business meet its goals, it must have three important elements:

Leaders need to be internally transparent. You can't be truthful with anyone else if you're lying to yourself.

Leaders must communicate transparency and constancy of purpose. Talk *with* the people, not *at* the people. Think about the message you're trying to convey, and be open to feedback about your message and how you're communicating it.

Finally, leaders need to model and expect business transparency: unfettered truth-sharing across the entire enterprise. Talk with a purpose, say what you're doing, and do what you say.

In the plant at Fayetteville, we were intentional with messaging a constancy of purpose. We held town hall meetings, sent out weekly newsletters, and had lunch information meetings with small groups of 15 people daily on all shifts. We also shut the plant down monthly to review results with all employees. The lost tires from the shutdown weren't a cost or profit loss: this was an investment.

As we talked with all of the plant's stakeholders, we varied our language but kept our meaning consistent. The language our C-suite management used wasn't the same language that was familiar and comfortable to our workers on the factory floor. We gave every constituent group the same information about the plant and its operations, in language tailored to that group's usual way of talking about the business.

Common language wasn't our goal; common meaning was. We wanted to be deliberately clear in the language of each culture. For instance, if we were talking to executives, we might have cited return on investment, percentage to scrap, EBITDA (earnings before interest, taxes, depreciation, and amortization), return on sales, purchase price value, and customer OTIF (on time in full) delivery. That's language people learn in business school—but you don't need a business school degree to understand the underlying concepts.

On the shop floor, we used a different narrative to create the same meaning. "Return on investment" became "cost to produce." "Percentage to scrap" is part of a conversation about minimizing waste. If we want no more than one percent to scrap, we can scrap a maximum of one of every 100 tires we produce. Go ahead and eat the first pancake of the batch, but the next 99 need to go to customers. I talked about profits and expenses in terms of customer orders, which produce revenue, and our production budget, which is the cost of creation that we deduct from revenue.

I had team and town hall meetings to explain how the plant was doing, teaching the business in a common language (Table 1.2). Graphs helped me get everyone on the same page around expectations and deliverables—or, in shop-floor language, what our factory was supposed to do and by when.

TABLE 1.2 Different Language, Common Meaning

EXECUTIVE SUITE LANGUAGE	MANAGEMENT LANGUAGE	SHOP FLOOR LANGUAGE	Interpretation
EBITDA	EBITDA	Profit or Loss	Same meaning
Material Variance	Waste as % Loss FSV	Scrap vs Units Produced	Same meaning
Asset Utilization	Output/Labor Efficiency	Units Produced to Goal	Same meaning

Real-life examples helped me get my message across:

- If you work 40 hours a week at $30 an hour, you earn $1,200 a week, or $4,800 a month.
- Your bills total $4,000 a month, leaving you with $800 to spend or save.
- But if I cut 25 of your hours because the factory doesn't have enough orders, then you have $3,000 a month to pay $4,000 in bills.

What will you cut: house, utilities, cars, insurance, vacation, college tuition? When we don't produce customer orders on time and in full, we as a company don't get paid, so we cut employee hours accordingly. That's profit and loss in a nutshell.

We found that, when people understood the gap between the factory's current performance and the performance we needed to see from it, they were enthusiastic about helping bridge that divide. People wanted to win.

Transparency and clear communication also helped us overcome opposition. Like most of Goodyear's tire plants, the Fayetteville factory was a union shop. The union traditionally had an adversarial relationship with plant management that had kept my predecessors and the organization from achieving success. Radical transparency is one of the ways I helped the union brass see the wisdom of working in concert with both employees and managers.

If I had told union leadership about my plans before I told employees, those officials would have gained an opportunity to put their own slant on my thoughts. Instead, I told everyone at the Fayetteville plant at the same time and invited the union leaders to all my meetings. Nothing was secret, and everything about the overall strategy came directly from me.

> **Every level of a business, from CEO to janitor, needs a connection to a strategy in order for that strategy to work.**

Communicating with the rest of the organization around strategy and goals is just the first step. Companies also need to indicate who is responsible for what part of the strategy. Every level of a business, from CEO to janitor, needs a connection to a strategy in order for that strategy to work. The connection needs to be specific. If we're going to bail out a leaking boat, one sailor needs to know that she is in charge of emptying buckets, and another should be aware that he is accountable for hooking up the pump. No one should be standing around feeling awkward.

P. J. Fleck, head football coach at the University of Minnesota, calls this "rowing the boat." In competitive rowing, everyone in the boat has a distinct role to play. Each person has a job to do. No one is dead weight.

CONSIDER THIS

As you finish this chapter, consider:

- How do you define winning for your organization?
- What needs to change for your organization to win?
- What's your organization's mission-critical goal? How do you know if you've reached that goal?
- What stakeholder groups are within your organization?
- How will you communicate transparently with each stakeholder group?
- What "ugly babies" might you need to call out?
- What other issues of transparency might you encounter?
- How can you communicate your strategy to everyone in your company?
- How can you earn the right to change?

CHAPTER 2

Developing Your Strategy

You understand your goal and critical performance indicator, and you're committed to transparent leadership. It's time to figure out how you'll all work to meet your organization's goals.

To do this, you'll use a purpose map (Figure 2.1). Also called SOAP, for "strategy on a page," a purpose map helps you figure out where you are, determine where you want to go, dig out the information you need to share, and begin to determine the actions that will get you there (Figure 2.2). You can use a purpose map for an entire organization or for just one aspect of operations: a department, a function, or even a single person's role in a business.

Without the information a purpose map contains, organizations flounder. They don't have a clear sense of what they're doing and why, and this situation tends to make people fearful. Fearful of making the wrong move, they don't make any move at all, and the business stagnates or simply reacts, putting out the biggest fire of the day without making any real progress toward its goals.

Understanding your purpose, goals, tools, and metrics makes the difference between finding your way through a dark cave with nothing more than the clothes on your back and navigating the same landscape with overhead lighting, a compass, and a map. It's the beginning of understanding where you are, where you want to go, and what actions will help you bridge the gap.

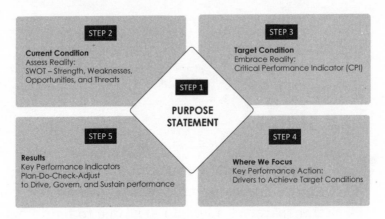

FIGURE 2.1 Components of a Purpose Map

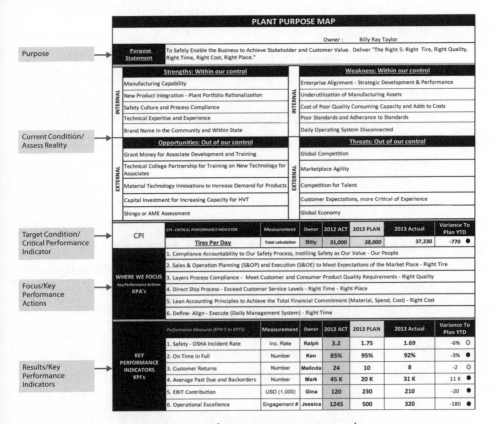

FIGURE 2.2 Plant Purpose Map Example
*(Throughout the print version of this book, wherever I have used
a green dot, it appears as white; red appears as black.)*

A purpose map begins with a purpose statement (Figure 2.3). An organization's purpose is the big picture version of why it exists. That Goodyear factory existed to make tires that fit Goodyear's quality standards as well as our customers' specifications, in quantities sufficient to meet our orders. Your organization has its own purpose.

| Purpose | → | Purpose Statement | To Safely Enable the Business to Achieve Stakeholder and Customer Value. Deliver "The Right 5: Right Tire, Right Quality, Right Time, Right Cost, Right Place." |

FIGURE 2.3 Purpose Statement

Be careful that you don't confuse your organization's purpose with its goals. Your company's purpose is over-arching and unchanging. Goals support that purpose. For instance, your nonprofit might exist to support research into kidney diseases: that's its purpose. It hopes to raise $3 million dollars this year to fund a particular research project: that's its current goal.

At the Fayetteville Goodyear plant, the goal that supported our purpose was making 38,000 tires a day. Again, those tires needed to meet Goodyear quality standards and customer specifications. That doesn't change. Our goals probably will change over time. If we have more orders, for instance, we might want to make more than 38,000 tires a day. If a new technology emerges, for instance, we might adapt our processes to use it.

A reality assessment is the next part of a purpose statement. Are we making 38,000 high-quality, on-specification tires a day? When I got to Fayetteville, the plant was turning out 30,000 to 31,000 of those tires every day. We had a gap between 7,000 and 8,000 tires. What issues were constraining us? Could we close that gap?

THE SWOT ANALYSIS: STRENGTHS, WEAKNESSES, OPPORTUNITIES, AND THREATS

A reality assessment includes a SWOT analysis (Figure 2.4), which considers an organization's strengths, weaknesses, opportunities, and threats. You could also do a SWOT analysis on something smaller than your entire organization: a division, a department, even a single person. Any entity that has a goal is eligible for this assessment.

FIGURE 2.4 SWOT Analysis

CRITICAL PERFORMANCE INDICATOR

After the SWOT analysis, identify what is the *critical performance indicator (CPI)* (Figure 2.5). This is the target condition or results that you want to accomplish. This is the critical indicator for an organization's existence.

FIGURE 2.5 Critical Performance Indicator

To begin, we need to know the goal and who we hope will accomplish it. That person or group's task is to bridge the gap between the current situation and the desired state of affairs.

KEY PERFORMANCE ACTIONS

The measures you take to bring your organization to where you want it are called *key performance actions* (Figure 2.6). What actions will you take to bring about a desirable change? Perhaps your child screams and yells for hours before bedtime. What measures—storybooks, a snack, a stuffed toy—might restore peace to your evenings?

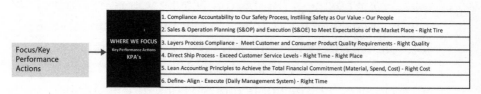

FIGURE 2.6 Key Performance Actions

You will also need to know how you'll find out whether or not you've met your goals. In Fayetteville, we looked at the number of high-quality, on-spec tires we completed every day. In the world of lean manufacturing, that metric is called our *key performance indicator*: the number we look at to see if we are meeting our goals as an organization. Yours might involve the number of customer service calls successfully handled every hour, ice cream cones served, or tantrums thrown. Is your toddler spending more or less time shrieking before bed?

Lastly, you'll look at results. Did the key performance actions do what you hoped they would? Look at your key performance indicator and find out. If yes, you can move on to the next set of circumstances you'd like to improve or set new goals for this key performance indicator. If the situation hasn't improved, or hasn't improved to the degree that you'd hoped, you'll need to try different key performance actions and review the results again.

KEY PERFORMANCE INDICATORS

A key performance indicator (Figure 2.7) is a quanti-fiable way to test your hypotheses about what might make your business run better. Maybe you think that issuing steel-toed boots to every employee will improve your plant's safety record. Hand out the boots and then measure your OSHA incident rate. If it's lower, there's a good chance that the boots did the trick. If the number doesn't move or gets higher, you need to try other ways to make your factory safer.

Results/Key Performance Indicators →

KEY PERFORMANCE INDICATORS KPI's

Performance Measures (KPA'S to KPI'S)	Measurement	Owner	2012 ACT	2013 PLAN	2013 Actual	Variance To Plan YTD	
1. Safety - OSHA Incident Rate	Inc. Rate	Ralph	3.2	1.75	1.69	-6%	O
2. On Time in Full	Number	Ken	85%	95%	92%	-3%	●
3. Customer Returns	Number	Melinda	24	10	8	-2	O
4. Average Past Due and Backorders	Number	Mark	45 K	20 K	31 K	11 K	●
5. EBIT Contribution	USD (1,000)	Gina	120	230	210	-20	●
6. Operational Excellence	Engagement #	Jessica	1245	500	320	-180	●

FIGURE 2.7 Key Performance Indicators
(In the print version of this book, green appears as white; red appears as black?

Key performance indicators (KPIs) also help organizations focus their attention on what matters most and make decisions with those target areas in mind. As the famous management consultant Peter Drucker said, "What gets measured gets done."

To use KPIs, set targets—the desired performance level—and track progress against that target. Managing with KPIs often means working to improve things now in order to reap benefits later.

Figure 2.8 illustrates how a purpose map works. It shows a chart of my efforts to lose weight. As you can see, my project has a purpose—to get healthy—and an overall goal: to lose 50 pounds. The reality is that I'm heavier than is ideal for my health. Then we get into the nuts and bolts of objective reality. What about me and my situation supports my purpose and goal? What could sabotage it?

Strengths: These are things I control that are working. I'm proud of them. On the supportive side, I like to eat salads and I know I need to make some changes. I have healthy, fit friends, and I played sports in college.

Weaknesses: These things constrain my project. On the minus side, I love to eat candy and I'm not particularly eager to exercise. My busy schedule makes it harder for me to commit to spending time working out. My job is sedentary, and I'm not fond of healthy, organic foods.

Opportunities: These are gifts and they can be game-changing. I have opportunities to get

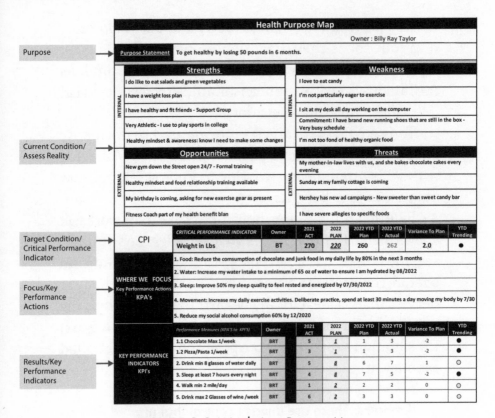

FIGURE 2.8 Weight Loss Purpose Map

fitter and lighter. There's a new gym down the street where I could get coaching about both fitness and food, and I have access to exercise equipment.

Threats: These can sink the boat. My mother-in-law's homemade chocolate cakes are a threat. So are the upcoming holidays, my severe allergies to some foods, and a new advertising campaign for my favorite kind of chocolate.

EXAMPLE: FAYETTEVILLE PLANT

A SWOT analysis of the Fayetteville plant demonstrates that, just like my weight-loss project, the tire factory had strengths and weaknesses, opportunities and threats.

Strengths

On the plus side, Fayetteville's leadership team had experience in manufacturing tires, with an average tenure of 20 years. They were knowledgeable about effective ways to product quality tires.

Fayetteville's communications systems and channels were also a strength. The communication manager was influential and respected. The plant's communications processes and platforms had worked well in the past. They could work for us again—but the team needed to communicate with deliberate clarity, tailoring their language to the audience. We had support from senior leadership. Corporate headquarters was committed to the change we wanted to see from the plant. The hourly workforce was strong, too, with plenty of experience and collective knowledge. When engaged, they were very productive. Last but certainly not least, the Fayetteville community was behind the plant's success. Fayetteville was a company town, and its people strongly supported Goodyear's operations there.

Weaknesses, Too

The Fayetteville plant also had weaknesses and threats. First among these weaknesses was the factory's adversarial culture. The place was divided into two teams: the salaried executives versus the union. The plant's culture had poor adherence to standards and contracts—even the union-negotiated contract. Rules existed, but no one seemed to be expected to follow them, not all of the time. Instead of determining a standard and sticking to it, people expected that management would always be ready to play Let's Make a Deal. In this aspect, management rarely disappointed them.

For instance, the plant rule was that workers needed to wear hard hats in designated areas. This regulation wasn't arbitrary or silly: tire factories can be dangerous places, and a person who isn't wearing appropriate protective gear can be hurt or killed. But workers at the plant were casual to the point of carelessness about where and if they wore hard hats. "But I was just on my way to my locker" was a typical excuse.

When I became plant manager, I had a white line painted on the floor between the locker area and the factory floor. If I caught someone on the floor without a hard hat, I wrote that person up. Workers had to walk by the locker area to reach their workstations, so they no longer had an excuse for not having appropriate protective gear.

In my experience, there is rarely a reason to deviate from holding to a standard. What you accept, you cannot change. Accepting workers' excuses about not wearing hard hats prevented the Fayetteville plant from creating an atmosphere where people routinely wore their protective gear. I have never found a reason why the standard should not have been the standard—period.

The Fayetteville facility also had poor operating processes and standards. Work instructions were often unclear. The operating system was ineffective, as was the daily management. Actions were poorly governed.

Even while some standards were ignored or left to happen or not according to whim, other jobs and processes were overmeasured, with far too many metrics for anyone to make sense of. Any attempt to focus on more than one metric at a time is challenging, at the very least. Meeting 10 or more metrics for a single task borders on the impossible. Sometimes the metrics conflicted, which made meeting them literally impossible.

> Every person who works there should understand a business's purpose, goals, and how it hopes to achieve these goals. No one should ever be in the dark about whether the company is accomplishing what it set out to achieve.

As you might expect from an organization that's this muddled, the Fayetteville factory wasn't nearly as transparent as it should have been. Organizations should clearly offer everyone the same information. Of course individuals have personal details that should stay private, but nothing about the rules of how the company runs should be secret. Every person who works there should understand a business's purpose, goals, and how it hopes to achieve these goals. No one should ever be in the dark about whether the company is accomplishing what it set out to achieve.

KEY PERFORMANCE INDICATORS AND ACTIONS

An honestly handled SWOT analysis gives you a fairly accurate picture of reality: you see the things we have going for and against us. Our next task is to consider how we will maximize our strengths and opportunities while also finding ways to overcome our weaknesses and threats.

Regarding my weight-loss plan, the number on the scale is my key performance indicator. If I give myself 25 weeks to lose 50 pounds, then I should lose two pounds a week. When I weigh myself at the end of each week, the number on the scale should be two pounds less than it was the week before. If I don't meet this performance indicator, then I know I am not on track to win.

In Fayetteville, net productivity was our key performance indicator. To determine our goal number, we kept track of just three things: parts produced per hour, parts scrapped, and how many hours of time were devoted to producing the first two numbers. I like to track key performance indicators on a chart. A green dot indicates that, for that metric, I am on track to win. A red dot indicates that I am not on track to win. There are no yellow dots. You are either on track or you're off track, with nothing in between. *(In the print version of this book, red dots will appear black, and green dots appear white.)*

Now I need to plan the actions that we think will help us move into and stay green. These key performance actions are the steps I will take that move me closer to my goal.

For example, to lose those 50 pounds, I plan to reduce my junk food and chocolate consumption by 80 percent, drink a minimum of 65 ounces of water every day, improve my sleep quality by 50 percent, make daily exercise a habit, and reduce my social alcohol consumption by 60 percent. I've indicated dates by which I will have made these changes so they don't stay in the vague and misty future.

What does that mean in very granular terms? It means that I can have chocolate and pizza or pasta once a week. It means that I need to drink eight glasses of water every day, sleep for seven hours each night, walk at least two miles every day, and drink no more than two glasses of wine every week. Those are my key performance actions and indicators. They tell me exactly what I need to do in order to make progress toward my goal. By tracking them, I create key performance indicators that clearly tell me what I must do and what I cannot do today.

Tracking them also lets me see the reasons for my success or failure. Those key performance actions themselves turn into goals, because either we are taking action or we are not. When we follow through on commitments to our key performance actions, they support our success. When we don't follow through on these key performance actions, they are leading candidates for the reasons behind our failure.

When I chart my weight loss project, it looks like Figure 2.9. My purpose map shows the following:

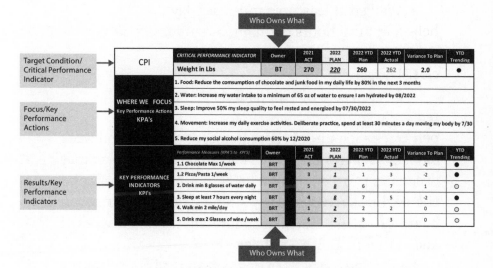

FIGURE 2.9 Key Performance Actions Linked to Key Performance Indicators

CPI Goal

- My goal is to lose 10 pounds, going from 270 pounds to 260 pounds.

Key Performance Actions (What Did I Plan?)

- Eat a maximum of one piece of chocolate per week
- Eat pizza or pasta not more than once a week
- Have a maximum of two glasses of wine a week
- Drink eight glasses of water per day
- Walk at least two miles per day
- Sleep for at least seven hours each night

Key Performance Indicators (What Did I Do?)

- Ate three pieces of chocolate per week
- Ate pizza and pasta three times per week
- Drank two glasses of wine per week
- Drank eight classes of water per day
- Walked at least two miles per day
- Slept five hours per night

CPI Actual

- Missed goal by two pounds

I track each one of these items, day by day and week by week. When I perform each of the key performance actions as planned, I put a green dot next to it. When I fall off the plan, whether by sleeping for less than seven hours or eating chocolate more than once a week, I assign that instance a red dot.

Reviewing the pattern of green and red dots gives me a lot of information:

All green dots. If all my dots are green, then I have met my goal, most likely by hitting my key performance actions. Hurrah!

Red at the top with the CPI and red with the key performance indicators. When there's a red dot next to my goal, I haven't achieved that goal. Red key performance indicators suggest that there's a good reason that I haven't reached it: I haven't followed through on my key performance actions. If I haven't lost two pounds this week, for instance, that might be because I've had chocolate three times (rather than the once that is my KPA), or because I haven't walked at least two miles every day. I need to try again next week to hit my KPAs. Writing down what I eat and how much I move could help me get a more exact idea of whether I'm really working the levers that can bring about change, or if I need to reassess my key performance actions.

Green at the top and red underneath. I met my goal, even though I didn't follow through with all my KPAs. This suggests two possibilities. Either the red KPAs aren't important—maybe I can afford to eat chocolate three times a week and still lose weight—or the goal is set too low. If I can lose two pounds in a week when I eat chocolate three times, I might lose three pounds in a week where I only eat chocolate once.

Red at the top and green underneath. I haven't met my goal, even though I've faithfully performed my KPAs. I don't see this happening very often. When it does, it's because I haven't chosen the right KPAs or because I'm not performing those KPAs as faithfully as I should. If this happened during a week of my weight-loss journey, perhaps I'd write down what I ate every day to be sure that I was really hitting those KPAs. Otherwise, I'd need to look for new KPAs. My initial choices aren't the right ones.

WHAT CAN GO WRONG WITH A PURPOSE MAP?

Purpose maps work, but they are not a fail-safe against human error or sidetracking. When I see a purpose map that isn't getting an organization closer to fulfilling its purpose and meeting its goals, I suspect that one of the following things has gone wrong:

They Lacked Purpose or Clarity Around Their Purpose

A business needs a purpose, and everyone involved with that business needs to know and understand that purpose. When an organization's purpose is clear, it aligns with long-term financial performance, provides a clear context for making daily decisions, and both motivates and unifies everyone who is a part of that organization.

A tire factory exists to make tires that meet the company's and customer standards for quality and satisfy clients' specifications and expectations. That may seem fairly obvious—but a surprising number of organizations lack a clear, easily understood, often-stated purpose. When a company has a clear purpose and everyone involved understands that purpose completely, making other decisions becomes much simpler.

They Lacked Clear Metrics

Next, companies need metrics that help them manage their responsibilities. Finding out the score is the first thing we do when we go to a sports event. Business shouldn't be any different. Don't just tell a worker that she is in charge of the buckets. Communicate to her that you expect her to achieve the standard by emptying six buckets a minute and give her a process and place to mark down every bucket she empties. How else will she know that she's meeting the standard and contributing appropriately to the group's success?

At this Goodyear factory, the people who actually made the tires had no reason to feel engaged. They didn't know what specific goals management had set for the business. They hadn't been given any roles in the process of meeting those goals, which fostered a lack of ownership and a work environment that was neither productive nor inclusive.

Even if someone had assigned them roles, they had no way to know if they were doing their jobs adequately. If you make five tires today, will that help the company get closer to its goal? Will 10 do the trick? You don't know—and neither did the people who worked in this tire factory.

They Had Too Many Metrics

Measuring what matters—and only what matters—is vital. Having no metrics is detrimental. Having too many metrics can be even worse because it can obscure what's important. If I tell you that you need to make 10 tires every day, that's clear and actionable. You can keep that number in your head. You can write it on a whiteboard. In a matter of seconds, you can determine how many tires you've made. You see the results of your effort.

At the Fayetteville plant, we needed to keep track of just three things: parts produced per hour, parts scrapped, and how many hours of time went into producing the first two numbers. We combine those three figures to learn our net productivity. We monitor just three things to come up with our key performance indicator! That's manageable.

Now imagine that I've asked you to keep track of how many tires you make and what time you arrived and left work—but I also want you to note the air temperature at your workstation, how many of your coworkers are wearing blue shirts, how much coffee the factory consumes every day, whether your team prefers regular or hazelnut-flavored creamer on any given day, and the phases of the moon. These are arbitrary metrics, of course, but you can see how tracking them would distract you from the metrics that matter: how much time you spent at work and how much you got done while you were there. The problem would be even worse if none of the metrics I asked you to measure had anything to do with your work.

Many companies expect their workers to track metrics that don't really matter, don't matter to the person assigned to track them, or are of significantly less importance than the metrics that really do matter. They fail to prioritize and focus on mission-critical information, and they don't link key performance indicators to key performance actions. No one can focus on 50 metrics (or

goals) and be genuinely effective, and a dashboard that focuses on too many is doomed to fail.

Their Metrics Were Disconnected from Their Actions

Metrics should be directly related to what an employee does (key performance actions) and should help workers and managers focus on how and what they achieve. Fundamentally, that's where strategic success lies.

When you have a purpose and metrics, combining the two gives you the strategy you need to reach your goals. For instance, let's say that your purpose is to support your family emotionally and financially. You determine that taking your family on a one-week vacation would be good for everyone's emotional life. To pay for the vacation you've chosen, you'll need $1,000. You have two months to save that money. $1,000 divided by 60 days is about $17 a day. To reach the goal that supports your purpose, you'll need to put away $17 every day for the next two months. If two people are doing the saving, each of them needs to contribute $8.50 to the envelope marked "vacation" every day.

The same math works for a tire factory. The factory's purpose is to make quality tires that fit customer specifications. Making 2,400 tires a day is the goal that supports that purpose. In a factory with (for instance) six divisions, each division needs to make 400 tires a day. If each division has 40 employees, then each employee is in charge of making 10 tires during the course of each eight-hour shift.

Now obviously tire factory math is more complicated than that—but you can see the principle. Determine an organization's purpose. Select goals that match that purpose. Use an organizational flow chart and simple math to figure out what each team member must contribute in order for the company to meet its goal.

A person who is clear about what responsibilities she owns and which metrics tell her whether she's meeting those responsibilities can use that information to make decisions. If you're saving for a vacation and you have $20 left in your wallet for today, you know that you can't go out to lunch and still meet your goal. If you make tires and you want to know if you can go to lunch, you have only to answer a single question: Have you made five tires yet today? If the answer is yes, then your day has reached its midpoint and you can find one of those refrigerators. It's lunchtime.

The Factory Had No Structured Daily Management

Let's say that this factory has 1,000 tire makers. I tell them all that each person needs to make 24 tires a day if we are to meet our company's goal.

Anyone who has spent time in any business of any size knows that there will be some glitches on the way to 1,000 people each making 24 tires a day. Machines might break. People might not adhere to policy or could have behavioral issues. The plant might not have enough of one or more raw materials. Workers might be confused about manufacturing specifications on a new product.

A daily management system is a set of processes and meetings, touch points through which team members evaluate their progress toward accomplishing strategic objectives. This system of regular meetings lets people compare notes and catch problems early, helping companies manage the things that need to be addressed on any given day. But at Fayetteville's Goodyear factory, managers didn't have a formal daily operating process to talk about how the plant would meet its goals and effectively eliminate constraints. The place ran on the squeaky wheel principle: whoever or whatever squeaked loudest got the attention. Unfortunately, the loudest person or thing wasn't necessarily the most important when it came to achieving performance targets.

Leadership Standards Were a Secret, Too

Making 38,000 tires a day is just one of the goals Fayetteville's Goodyear factory had. Those tires also needed to be of acceptable quality to both Goodyear and the factory's clients.

What makes a tire's quality acceptable? For that matter, what makes a sandwich or a shoe, a plate of oysters or a tuba lesson good enough? The standard must be clear to everyone. At many (but not all) organizations, someone knows the answer. But as with organizational goals, the standards are sometimes a secret. They aren't widely, clearly known throughout the company.

Organizations fail because they don't have standards, because people don't know the standard, or because they have poor operational and leadership standards. Sometimes that failure happens because a factory makes lousy tires. Without standards, what you get is "round and black and out the back."

In other circumstances, the problem around standards is both less obvious and more pervasive. Leadership standards shape organizational culture. They influence people. Leaders who successfully lead change for organizational effectiveness do it by influence rather than by authority. When you have high, nonnegotiable standards, you become a magnet. People want to follow skilled, ethical leaders who treat other people well, no matter where in the organizational chart those people fall. The janitor from that plant in Fayetteville is still a good friend of mine.

Effective leadership is less about your title and more about your moral and ethical values and actions. People follow leaders they trust and respect; both attributes take a long time to earn and only a second to lose. Your job title might give you authority, but your standards and ethics demonstrating those actions give you the right to lead.

Leaders Hadn't Earned the Right to Change Things

Everyone wants to lose weight and stay healthy, but no one wants to hire a trainer who will make us eat less or exercise more. Organizational change works the same way. Human beings are slow to cooperate with those who would make us change.

Company executives might think that they have the right to change things at work. After all, the executives hire and fire the workers. They own the machinery and pay the bills. Leaders who provide resources—operating tools, assets, processes to move products through technological conversion—often feel they have earned the right to demand change for the better: increased efficiency, lower costs, innovative products and processes, and enhanced company value.

It's true that technical change contributes to how organizations deliver customer, employee, and overall business value. But by itself, it is not enough. Unfortunately, the technical right to change will not win hearts and minds. You'll get (at best) a grudging response, not the full-blown enthusiasm you need to take an operation from failing to fully meeting its goals and purpose.

For that, you have to earn the cultural right to change, which is about behavior, environment, and communication. People don't change because of technical changes, or even because change is the logical choice. First, they need to embrace change.

Cultural change isn't something that can be imposed from above. March in and give the people their marching orders, and new behaviors will last for as long as you're around to enforce them. A collaborative cultural change, on the other hand, goes viral. It's what gives an organization cultural norms that stick long after you've moved on to your next professional adventure.

Think about a college that has a culture that consistently emphasizes sororities and fraternities, football, basketball, practical jokes, or special traditions, like Harvard's Hasty Pudding Club or Yale's secret clubs. Most students don't spend more than four years at college, so the culture doesn't endure for decades because the same people remain there to support it. The students that prop up that culture leave on a predictable schedule.

Instead, two things happen: the college attracts people who want a school that emphasizes those special qualities, and the culture that celebrates those attributes gets passed along virally from one student to another. A new college president could make some changes but probably couldn't issue an edict that changed a college from a place famed for its quirky sense of humor to one renowned for its devotion to football. It just wouldn't work.

The same is true of your workplace. You can't successfully impose a new culture by fiat. You can't do it *to* your team. You have to do it *with* your team.

DEPLOYING THE STRATEGY

After the big picture strategy is formed, deploying and connecting the strategy is vital for success (Figure 2.10). The strategy should be broken down and aligned—both vertically and horizontally throughout the organization—embedded in an organization's functions and tiers. Following the same steps in purpose mapping, strategic deployment enables the enterprise to cascade the high-level plan (the strategy) and link the utilization of that strategy by employees for a deliberate purpose to achieve the critical performance indicators.

> **The strategy should be broken down and aligned— both vertically and horizontally throughout the organization— embedded in an organization's functions and tiers.**

MOVING FORWARD

You have talked with yourself and other people about the ways that your organization is falling short. You have a goal and a critical performance indicator. You understand how to earn both the technical and the cultural right to change. You have committed to transparent leadership and developed a SOAP analysis, using it to develop strategies that will bring your organization closer to its goals. You are ready for the next chapter, where you'll learn how your organization can align to win.

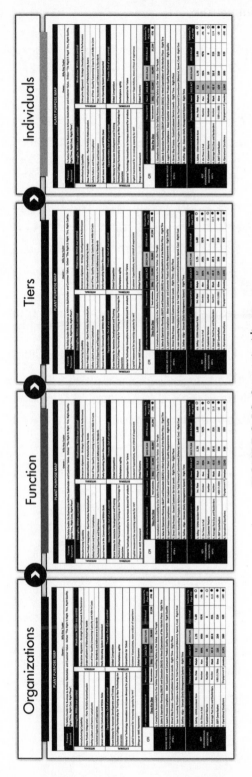

FIGURE 2.10 Strategic Alignment

CONSIDER THIS

As you finish this chapter, consider:

- What strengths, weaknesses, opportunities, and threats does your organization have?
- How will you build on the strengths and opportunities and minimize or avoid weaknesses and threats in ways that can help your company reach its most important goal?
- What's your overall strategy for organizational transformation?
- In what ways do you have the technical right to change?
- What will you need to do to earn the cultural right to change?
- How might you need to change as a leader to maximize your organization's chance of winning?

CHAPTER 3

Aligning to Win

n any organization, the formula for winning is simple. Strategy plus execution equals success (Figure 3.1).

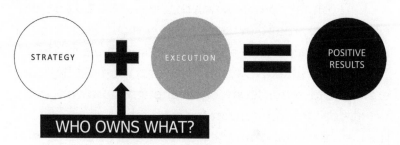

STRATEGY + EXECUTION = POSITIVE RESULTS

WHO OWNS WHAT?

FIGURE 3.1 Formula for Success

So why don't organizations with developed strategies win? Most of the time, it's because they aren't aligned around their strategy. Individuals don't understand what the key performance actions and indicators mean to them and how they spend their time at work. Like musicians in an orchestra, they need to know what bars of a symphony they're supposed to play so that the organization as a whole can make music.

EXTREME CLARITY AROUND INDIVIDUAL OWNERSHIP

Problems can happen when teams know what they need to do, but individual expectations aren't crystal clear. When I first arrived at the Fayetteville plant, we developed a great strategy and people were eager to execute that strategy. Managers' computer screens were full of reports featuring red and green dots—mostly green. We should have been getting results, but we weren't. Why wasn't the formula working?

Our primary problem was that we hadn't taken deliberate clarity around ownership far enough. People didn't know what tasks they alone were responsible for doing.

For the LinkedXL system to work, we must be deliberately and relentlessly clear about who owns what. What does winning mean for each job at every level of the organization, from the janitor to the CEO? It is vital to boil the strategy down to actionable items. When I arrived in Fayetteville, management was focused on the goal of making a certain amount of profit. That's fine, but "earn a 10 percent profit" (for instance) is a key performance indicator, not a key performance action. You can't instruct your employees to "do" a 10 percent profit.

If we have 10 tire machines and 10 machine operators, and we want to make 1,000 tires every day, we need each machine operator to make 100 tires. That's simple math—or it is when you tell each machine operator that you need that person to make 100 tires. But when you tell the team as a whole that you need 1,000 tires every day, without specifying how many tires each team member should make, something else happens. One person works very hard and makes 150 tires. Several people work about as much as you hoped they would and make 100 tires each. Some people may slack off and make 50 tires each.

That lack of ownership has one of two potential outcomes. Maybe the team manages to build 1,000 tires every day this week, and the manager is happy, congratulating the team for its good work. Or maybe the team falls short of its goal, and the manager scolds the group for not making the required number of tires. In either case, someone is either getting credit for work he didn't do or enduring criticism for work that she did do. The manager doesn't tell the person who made 50 tires a day that this is not an adequate effort. He gets the idea that 50 tires is a perfectly acceptable contribution. The person who made 150 tires a day, annoyed that the manager doesn't recognize this outsized accomplishment, quickly decides that it's not worth it to work very hard, since she could have made 50 tires a day without punishment, and the result of her effort is either silence or criticism. She dials down her efforts.

> **We must be deliberately and relentlessly clear about who owns what. What does winning mean for each job at every level of the organization, from the janitor to the CEO?**

Very soon, the entire team is making 50 tires a day. And why not? You didn't tell the team members what workload they each specifically owned. Companies fail when they don't take their strategy all the way down to the individual level.

Don't just stop at the team level. Take the time to figure out what each individual needs to do every day in order to support the overall strategy. Some teams will be full of people who each need to make the same daily contribution, as with my example of 10 workers making 1,000 tires a day. Other employees will have more specific, individual requirements. Either way, it's vital that you align your strategy, telling people exactly what they need to do every day in order to win at every level: as individuals, as team members, and as an organization.

OWNERSHIP BEATS ACCOUNTABILITY

It's vital that each individual understand what he or she needs to do to win both personally and as an organization. It's better still that individuals feel invested in their parts in the organization's symphony.

Many organizations look to keep workers accountable for their goals. Sell this much, bill that many hours, and you'll get a bonus. Fall short and you'll be disciplined or maybe even fired. That's accountability. I understand that there are things I need to do and consequences for either doing or not doing them.

But accountability isn't the same as ownership. If I own my part in the symphony, I don't just understand what I need to do and the consequences of my actions or inaction; I have gone past that level and I am taking my job personally. I care about the work I do. I am looking for methods to improve my performance by making my job better or more efficient. I might even devise ways to improve not just my job, but the effect that my work has on the company as a whole.

To understand the difference between accountability and ownership, think about what happens when you rent a car. You're accountable for that car. If you wreck it, the rental company will ask you (or your insurance company) to pay for the damage. Fail to bring it back on time, and eventually, the rental company will call the police and report you for theft.

But even though you're accountable for that car, you don't act like an owner. You probably aren't too fussy about what grade of fuel you put in a rental car, and you don't vacuum the upholstery. You put your feet on the seats. You let your kids eat in the car.

That's the difference between accountability and ownership. A person who clocks in, works simply to earn a bonus or earn enough money to keep the lights on at home, and clocks out is not engaged and involved to the degree that a worker who feels that he owns his job. The owner is the person who is motivated to do the job well and keep looking for ways to improve.

Keep in mind, too, that what people expect from their jobs has changed over the generations. My great-grandparents lived to work. They lived and worked on a farm, and the work they did there was their life. My parents worked to live. They got jobs to pay the bills, to put food on the table and a roof over our heads, and to put money aside for my future college expenses.

My children work and live. The trend was already toward trusting employees to be accountable for their own work. The Covid-19 pandemic, which forced many people to work from home instead of from an office filled with other employees, accelerated that trend. Working remotely, bosses had to influence rather than direct. Micromanagement became less of an option; employees had to own their work to succeed.

The pyramid is the traditional schematic for an organization that has one person in charge and many people executing that person's vision at multiple levels. A whole organization full of people who are the CEOs of their own roles within that company turns the pyramid on its head. Those employees then become the driving force behind that business's ultimate success.

Persuading people to take ownership of their jobs was a substantial challenge for me in Fayetteville. Some of the people there already owned their jobs. Some of them at least understood that they were there to work. But the factory was also full of people who had turned *not* working into an art form. They napped behind stacks of tread. They hid in sheds, bullied each other, got high or drunk at work.

During a walk through the plant with the Fayetteville union president, I asked him approximately many people worked in the factory. "Honest answer?" he replied. "About half of them."

There are dangers to running an operation like that, and suboptimal performance isn't the worst of them. The plant's existence was in danger. We needed to stop fighting about union grievances and secure people's jobs by making the plant one of the best in the industry. I showed the union president Goodyear's comparison of all its plants in North America. We were at the bottom of every performance category: safety, quality, cost, and performance. "Which one would you close next if you owned the company?" I asked him. "I know which one I would close, based on the facts." We didn't need to agree on everything, but we did need to work together to make positive changes if we wanted Fayetteville to have a Goodyear plant.

DO CHANGE *WITH* THE PEOPLE, NOT *TO* THE PEOPLE

At the Fayetteville Goodyear plant, developing a winning strategy took one month; that strategy then evolved over six months. At the end of six months, I had two things: an overall strategy for the plant that would let us win and a large group of workers who knew little or nothing of this strategy.

Not only was the strategy a secret—who owned what in the strategy was also a secret. Workers might have been excited and engaged to participate if they'd known about it—or they might have been entirely content to ignore the new strategy and keep doing things the way they'd always done them. Unless I got smart and proactive about communicating my strategy from the top of the plant to the bottom, from executives to hourly workers, we would never know.

Why can it be so difficult to get a large group of people excited and invested in a change process? The answer isn't that Americans don't like change or that we're disinterested in making life more efficient. The popularity of meal kits, Amazon orders, and TaskRabbit services suggest that we love making things faster, easier, or cheaper. We love change—when we think that we're the people choosing to change. We do not like having change imposed on us from above. In groups at work, people tend to feel cultural ownership of a place. In our minds, that's just as important—or even more important—than actual ownership of a business.

Workers know that their employer can fire them. They understand that a thriving business is in their best interest, because firms that are doing well can retain employees and pay them market-rate wages, and because it's also much more fun to work in a happy, successful place.

It's logical, then, for workers to want to get behind a strategy that will help their company thrive. That's exactly what you want your people to do. Yet it can be agonizingly difficult to get a workforce on board with a new strategic plan.

AVOID SINGLE-OWNERSHIP SYNDROME

In many organizations, 5 percent of the people—typically in senior leadership—believe that they make everything in the company happen in what can be called the accountability pyramid (Figure 3.2). Fifteen percent of the people attentively watch the senior leaders direct and dictate, with the expectation that they'll carry out the orders. The final 80 percent of people just wait for someone to tell them what to do. In that situation, only the top 5 percent really own anything.

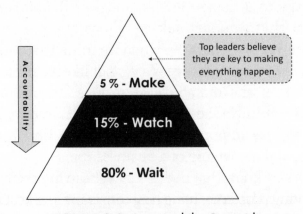

FIGURE 3.2 Accountability Pyramid

A similar phenomenon, called single-ownership syndrome, happens when companies appoint a single person in charge of change. Sometimes that's someone with a formal title; other times the job falls to the person who came up with the new strategy, the site manager, or the CEO. It's appropriate for a company to have leadership, of course, and directing change is a huge task, so designating someone to conduct the orchestra as it transitions from Bach to Berlioz, metaphorically speaking, is a reasonable thing to do.

The problem occurs when the company forgets that the change agent's job is to get everyone involved and invested in making the new strategy work. Instead, the company sees that leader as entirely responsible for creating the change. In reality, a designated person can lead the charge, but she can't make an entire organization do things differently. For that, a company needs virtually everyone, in every function and at every level, to invest in and commit to change.

Unless the change process quickly involves everyone at the organization, it stays on the change agent's desk. The rest of the company doesn't see any reason to change. That's someone else's problem. No one person can play all the roles in setting up a company to win, any more than one person can play all the parts in a movie or all the instruments in an orchestral performance.

Look at what happens when we use the LinkedXL process to flip that first situation on its head using the ownership pyramid (Figure 3.3). Now we have 80 percent of the people making things happen by executing the strategy. Fifteen percent are enabling that strategy by solving problems, removing constraints, and bringing the workforce what it needs to get the job done. The last

5 percent are the visionaries, providing clarity around purpose and goals.

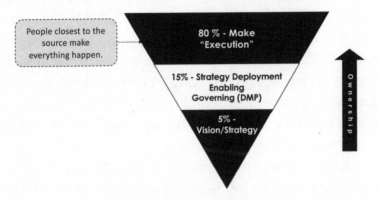

FIGURE 3.3 Ownership Pyramid

This switch was crucial to success in Fayetteville. Before I arrived, the company installed a new plant manager every two years. Each of those plant managers were the single and only agents of change in the plant, and not one of them ever got traction. Then I showed up and implemented extreme ownership (Figure 3.4). When people know what they own, they work in concert.

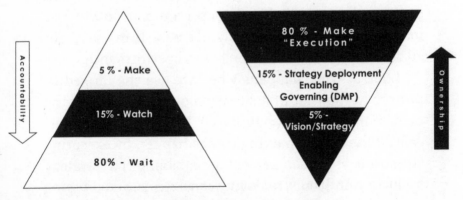

FIGURE 3.4 Extreme Ownership

To really understand the difference, imagine that you need to get a racing scull down the river. The boat has room for eight rowers and one coxswain, whose job it is to steer the boat and coordinate the rowers' efforts. It's the coxswain's job to get the team warmed up before practice, emphasizing points that the coach has focused on previously. The coxswain diagnoses problems and coaches the crew into taking corrective action, encourages the rowers, spots and fixes individual and team errors, and leads the celebrations when a rower's performance improves.

That's an important job. Yet no team has ever won a race by letting the coxswain steer, diagnose problems, coach fixes, celebrate improvements, and do all the rowing by herself. The eight rowers in the boat have to work in concert with the coxswain and with each other if the boat is to have any chance of outdoing the competition. Every athlete has a role in a winning boat.

PURSUE MEANINGFUL WORK

"Bisy, backson," reads the note that Christopher Robin left for his friends in A. A. Milne's classic children's book *The House at Pooh Corner*. (Christopher Robin means to say "Busy, back soon.") Everyone enjoys how being busy feels. We rush around, full of effort, feeling purposeful and important. Look how much we got done!

There's just one problem with this: the work we got done might not be meaningful work. In Fayetteville, the motto was "round and black and out the back." Production targets were vague, so employees did busywork, creating more inventory than clients had ordered.

Maybe we needed 200 pieces of tire tread. They'd make 300 pieces of tread and get paid for the time they spent doing it. The factory didn't have storage space, so employees tossed the extra into a recycling bin.

Sometimes they'd end up making yet more tread just a few hours later. Goodyear paid for the materials and time they spent making it, but the expenditure subtracted from the bottom line and occupied time and effort that could have been put to better use.

> Everyone enjoys how being busy feels. We rush around, full of effort, feeling purposeful and important. Look how much we got done!

I replaced that motto with continuous flow supply-chain management. The factory ran what the customers wanted, when and how they wanted it. Workers stopped wasting motion, time, and materials.

Teams and individuals need standards and a yardstick to measure them by. Simply telling the workers in Fayetteville to make more or better tires is a little like telling someone to jump without telling them how high. Standards tell us where we're aiming. Yardsticks tell us how close we're coming to our goal.

Measurable standards also give people opportunities to recognize key performance actions when they see them. Really understanding a goal in a measurable way helps workers see the obstacles to reaching that goal. Seeing the obstacles is the first step toward overcoming them.

Think back to the weight-loss example in my purpose map. If I know that I should eat pizza no more than once a week, I might notice that my daily walk around the neighborhood takes me past my favorite pizza parlor and its delicious (and tempting) smells. I now know that reaching my goal will be easier if I take a different route on most days. That's a new key performance action—one I might not have known about when I made my first purpose map for this project.

A culture of busyness can also create the belief that we, both as individuals and as a group, do not have enough time to rethink how we do our work. We spend our days doing what's urgent—and pretty much everything is urgent. When we make it safe to slow down and think, we create the space people and organizations need to do what's important, rather than merely what's urgent.

OWNERSHIP MAPPING

It's not easy to keep a list of every employee's responsibilities in your head. If your organization has more than a scant handful of employees, it is probably also impossible to even remember what everyone is supposed to do. You need to write it down.

A tire factory has thousands of employees working across multiple tiers and functions. To keep track of all the roles, I built an ownership map: a diagram of the plant's jobs that looked a little like a family tree. It was essentially an organizational chart, but with greater detail and additional information.

Every organization has multiple functions: human resources, operations, safety, and so forth. An individual manager oversees each function. Under that manager are more people, each with specific job responsibilities;

yet more people typically answer to those middle managers. Ironically, the people who actually do the work are usually at the bottom level.

Every person in every job on this chart has clear work to do and goals to meet. To align around the overall organization's critical performance target, we determine what part of that performance each person must shoulder and add that information to the ownership map. If we know that a plant should make 38,000 tires every day, and the plant has three shifts of 1,000 workers each, then simple math tells us that every shift needs to make 12,666 tires and every worker must make 38 tires.

> ∞
> **What actions are we going to take? How will we know if they're working?**

Every job, from the CEO to the janitor, contributes to the plant's ultimate goal: making 38,000 high-quality tires that meet customer specifications, every day.

Just as in my weight-loss example, we derive key performance actions and key performance indicators from our analysis of what the critical performance indicator means for each employee. What actions are we going to take? How will we know if they're working? To align around the KPAs and KPIs for which each person is responsible, we add that information to the ownership map.

If I commit to eating pizza just once a week, I can note whether or not I've taken that action. A green card indicates that I'm on plan for that key performance action. If I've fallen off the wagon and had pizza more than once, that key performance action gets a red card.

A weekly weigh-in reveals the key performance indicator. To lose 50 pounds in 25 weeks, I need to shed 2 pounds every week. Again, successful weeks are marked in green; unsuccessful weeks are marked in red. There is no yellow. Either I succeeded or I didn't. "Close" counts in horseshoes and atomic bombs, but not in my version of lean process management.

If my weekly weight check reveals that I'm in the green, I look at my key performance actions. There's a good chance that every one of those is also green. If one is red, then I might want to reconsider its place among key performance actions. Maybe it is not an important part of reaching my goal after all.

But if my weekly weight check shows that I haven't lost at least 2 pounds, I'm in the red, and one of two things is true. The most likely reason that I haven't met my goal is that I didn't meet a key performance action—which is also in the red. That's a lot of words to describe something that is easy to see in just a few seconds on a purpose map (Figure 3.5).

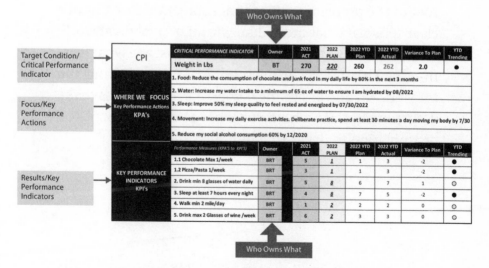

FIGURE 3.5 Weight-Loss KPA to KPI

If every job is a series of actions, it follows that when the factory as a whole isn't performing as it should, it's because someone in the group isn't doing the work they need to do for the group to succeed. As a manager, though, I didn't have the time to search the plant every day, looking for the person who was building 9 tires instead of 10. I needed a GPS grid system that would pinpoint the location of constraints and productivity roadblocks quickly and exactly.

With a purpose map, it takes me or anyone else about 10 seconds to see where the plant is winning and where it is not and who owns what. Moreover, we can drill down to the problem just as quickly. Any position that's marked with a red card in isolation is red because that person isn't meeting the job's key performance indicators—but it's more often true that red cards appear in groups. People aren't fully meeting the demands of their jobs because they aren't getting what they need from someone else. When that's the case, the root of the problem is often that someone doesn't have a clear sense of what individual winning involves at work.

Figures 3.8–3.10 illustrate how to cascade what winning is (Critical Performance Indicator), breaking the target down and assigning ownership. These steps make it extremely clear who owns what at every level of the organization to drive accountability for results.

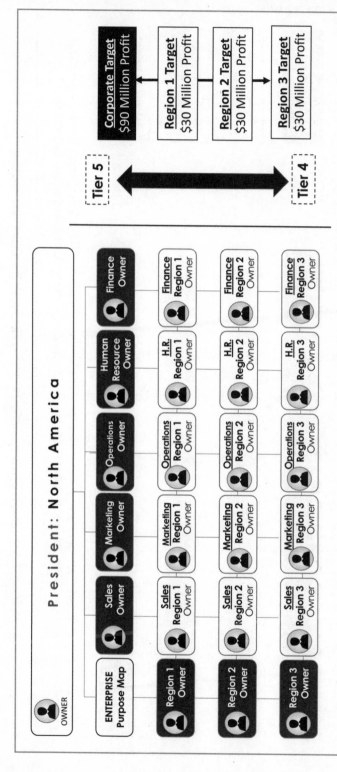

Tier 5 North America Owner and the Corporate functional owners responsible for $90 Million are connected to **Tier 4** Regional Owners (including functions) responsible for their contribution. **(Region 1: $30 Million) + (Region 2: $30 Million) + (Region 3 $30 Million) = Corporate $90 Million**

FIGURE 3.6 Ownership Map of Functions of North America Organization

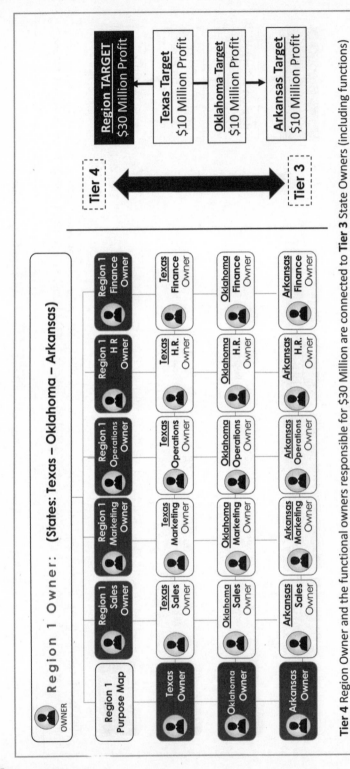

FIGURE 3.7 Ownership Map of Functions and Tier Levels (Functions and Regions)

Tier 4 Region Owner and the functional owners responsible for $30 Million are connected to **Tier 3** State Owners (including functions) responsible for their contribution. **(Texas $10 Million) + (Oklahoma $10 Million) + (Austin $10 Million) = State $30 Million**

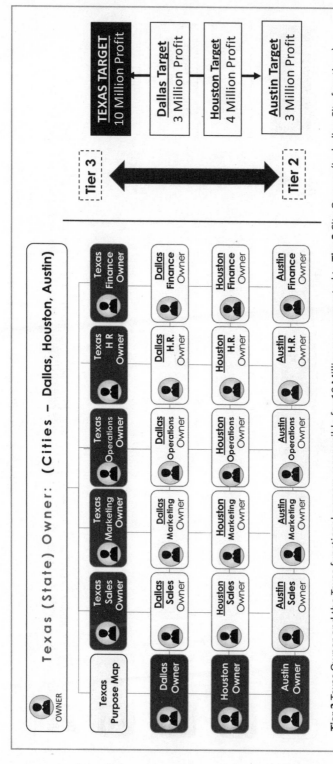

FIGURE 3.8 Ownership Map of Texas

Tier 3 Texas Owner and the Texas functional owners responsible for 10 Million are connected to **Tier 2** City Owners (including City functions) responsible for their contribution to the same total . **(Dallas $3 Million) + (Houston $4 Million) + (Austin $3 Million) = City $10 Million**

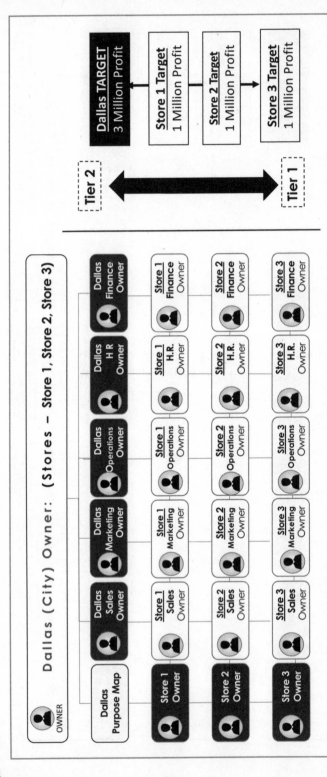

FIGURE 3.9 Ownership Map of Dallas

Tier 2 Dallas Owner and the Dallas functional owners responsible for $3 Million are connected to **Tier 1** Store Owners (including functions) responsible for their contribution to the same total. **(Store 1 = $1 Million) + (Store = $1 Million) + (Store 3 $1 Million) = Dallas $3 Million**

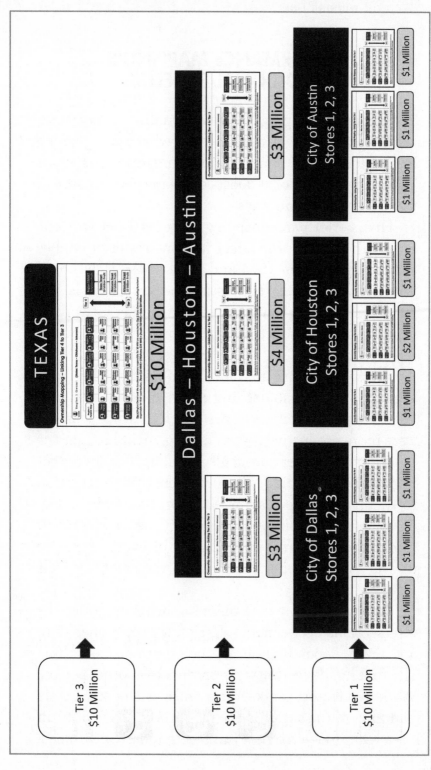

FIGURE 3.10 Ownership Mapping Texas Connected Enterprise View

PERFORMANCE MAPPING'S
ADDITIONAL BENEFITS

Performance mapping helps us visualize an organization and offers a way to zero in on what's going wrong in a business. But it's more than an organizational chart and a diagnostic tool. It boosts company performance in two other important ways.

First, performance mapping produces the Hawthorne effect. The Hawthorne effect was one result of studies conducted between 1924 and 1932 at the Hawthorne Works, a Western Electric factory in Cicero, Illinois. The Hawthorne Works wanted to study whether its workers would be more productive with more or less light on the factory floor.

The study didn't answer that question, though it arguably noticed something much more interesting. When management brought the lights up, workers were more productive. When management brought the lights down, worker output also went up. Employees got more done when the researchers were paying attention to them, and output slumped when the study ended. Performance mapping makes everyone important. It tracks the goals and performance of every employee in every job. No one falls through the cracks or feels invisible.

Second, performance mapping helps us notice the intersections between jobs. Very few people operate in a vacuum, depending on no one else to do something else first nor delivering work product to another person. Work in a factory is like a relay race, with participants handing off the baton as the race proceeds. It's difficult for a team to overcome a fumbled handoff with speed.

To win, a team must field fast athletes and have impeccable intersections between race segments.

The same is true of most businesses. For instance, good tread is an important tire component, but unless the tread maker communicates closely with the workers who create the other parts of a tire, the team won't work in harmony. Employees must talk with and listen to each other to maximize group performance.

Employees also need good relationships with company leaders. Even though this may not be a very close or personal relationship, depending on the size of the organization, all employees need to feel that they are valued and appreciated.

> ⌘ **Employees must talk with and listen to each other to maximize group performance.**

I decided in Fayetteville that when other people got within a few feet of me at work, I'd say hello to them—"the six feet rule." At first I was introducing myself; after a while I was saying hello to people I'd already met, then I was checking in with acquaintances, and eventually I was continuing conversations with friends. No one likes to feel invisible. I remember taking a potential hire on a tour, and he asked me, "Do you shake everyone's hand?" I said that yes, if they get within six feet of me, I shake their hand. "No way," he replied, "that's not for me. If they want to talk to me, they can come to me, and I am not shaking their nasty hands." I asked him if he had heard of soap. You can wash your hands later, but now is the time to create positive connections with your people.

CONSIDER THIS

As you finish this chapter, consider:

- Who owns what in your overall strategy for organizational transformation?
- How will you connect people to what they own?
- Work out a performance map that's similar to the one I made for my weight-loss journey for a personal goal of your own.
- Do teams and individuals know what they own in the strategy?
- Are roles and responsibilities clear in the organization's structure?
- Does creating this ownership map give you insight into how a performance map for your organization might look? Sketch out a rough version of that ownership map.
- What about your job do you own? Are there elements of your job for which you could be more clearly responsible? Modeling clarity and ownership around your role helps other people do the same for themselves.

CHAPTER 4

Cultivating Ownership

When people don't know what they own, they tend to blame others when something goes wrong or expectations aren't met. Think about taking a teenager's car keys when the kid misses curfew. The first words out of my teenager's mouth would have been, "Dad, that's not fair." If he didn't know what he was accountable for, he would blame his parents when things went sideways.

When my then-teenage son got a car, I was very clear about his key performance actions and key performance indicators. To keep the car, he needed to earn a grade of at least B in every class, be home by midnight, and volunteer for community service for at least five hours a month.

> In the absence of ownership comes blame.

When he missed his curfew, I took the keys. I later came into the kitchen to find him negotiating and debating with his mother. I told him that the standard is the standard; he lost his car keys because of a choice he made. He understood what he owned. As his parent, my job was to hold him to the standard. I know that things happen. Cars break down; friends need rides home. In that case, however, he should have called me or his mother first. Standards are not monuments, but they are the core of consistency. All my children had the same standard when they received a car. I made it very clear what they owned and what their mother and I owned. (We owned the payment, insurance, and maintenance.)

TAILOR YOUR COMMUNICATION TO YOUR AUDIENCE

Just like my son, employees need their leaders to be deliberately and relentlessly clear about what each job entails at every level of the organization, as well as about who owns what. I started doing this in Tyler, messaging up and down the ladder about who owns what in every part of the plant's business strategy.

I learned several things about clarity during my two years in Texas. First, it's vital to boil the strategy down to actionable items. When I arrived, management was focused on the goal of making a certain amount of profit. That's fine, but "earn a 10 percent profit" (for instance) is a key performance indicator, not a key performance action.

You can't "do" a 10 percent profit; however, you can transform a culture, in part by being very clear as you define both individual and group success. When I do this, I tailor the language to the audience, using different words to arrive at a common meaning.

I remember taking my son to a park in the 'hood in Dallas to play basketball. Guys I knew from growing up were there and greeted me with high fives and "Yo, B, what's up?" That's not how I greet people at the office, where handshakes and "Hello, I'm Billy Taylor" are the norm. But both "Yo, B!" and "Hello, Billy," mean "friendly greetings," even though they use different words.

The financial experts at Goodyear responded when I talked to them about earnings before interest, taxes, depreciation, and amortization, or EBITDA—a common measurement of corporate financial health. The people on the factory floor knew nothing about EBITDA but were fluent in the language of machine settings and tread widths. Figure out the language that your audience uses and adopt that way of communicating as you explain individual and company goals.

CLARITY IS A SPRINGBOARD TO CONTINUOUS IMPROVEMENT

When people understand what they own and what you expect of them individually and as a group, they know exactly where they stand. Imagine that I tell you I want you to make 10 tires every day and that those tires need to meet both client specifications and Goodyear's standards for quality. You don't need to wonder where you stand with me. If you are making 10 tires a day as described, then you are doing a great job and have nothing to worry about.

A mind that's free from wonder and worry has bandwidth left over to look around and see what could be better. Workers who got good at consistently making their tire quotas every day started to think that maybe their jobs would be easier if they moved their tools closer to their workbenches. They might be able to make an extra tire every now and then if they didn't have to wait for materials to arrive from the central storage point. Having two people reset two machines might be faster and more accurate than having each person reset one machine.

That kind of creativity is exactly what you want. There's no way that I, or any other manager, can know every detail of every job in a factory. You can't be everywhere, pointing out instances where a change would be an improvement. As a group, individual workers can. Once you've shown them that continuous improvement benefits everyone, your message goes viral.

Every key performance action is performed by an individual, and improvements happen because individual workers practice the actions that, taken together, move the key performance indicators. When you break down individual job components, workers can see additional actions they could take that would improve performance even more.

They take ownership of those actions and they're no longer cogs in a machine, subject to the whims of people above them and with no real interest in how the things they do contribute to the company's success or failure. Individual workers are genuine CEOs of the portion of the business that stands before them, and they can see how regular, consistent effort creates measurable change.

There's probably no need to measure every key performance action unless measurement is an important part of getting the action right. (I'm imagining a mixture that needs to be cooked at a precise temperature, or a surface that needs to be hit at an exact 45-degree angle.) Giving feedback on key performance actions can be helpful, though, as long as it's presented as encouragement and neutral information. No one in the midst of learning new things needs extra stress or criticism.

Give people the support they need to do new things well, including time to learn and practice, and avoid assigning blame. Individual blame leads to hesitation, withdrawal, and holding back—exactly the behavior that we want to reduce as we move people toward feeling more engaged, empowered, and responsible.

TRUST THE EXPERTS

Managers who want ideas about how to improve the ways that workers handle a particular job should probably talk to the experts: the people who spend 8 to 10 hours a day actually doing that work. They're the folks who know what's possible now and what more they would need to fuel different outcomes.

To me, that's logical: I'm astonished by the managers who think they know better than the janitor does about the most effective brand of floor polish or what time the dumpsters get emptied. Yet, the world is full of C-suite executives who design improvement plans for jobs they've never done, dealing with levels of detail that they simply don't have the time or expertise to manage.

I saw this all the time at Goodyear, where people routinely managed at least two levels below the point where they should have been managing. Instead of directing the orchestra, the band leader was trying to play every instrument. As a result, they often came up against problems they knew nothing about solving. I noticed that the same thing happened to me: my manager's manager directed me.

During a plant visit, an executive directed the plant manager to remove 10 of the plant's older-style manufacturing machines because the plant had purchased five new, high-technology tire machines. The new machines were slower than the old ones, but they required half the manpower to operate.

The hourly team lead tried to tell him that removing the machines was a mistake. The executive yelled and cursed at the team lead for having the temerity to contradict him. He was an executive! Of course he was in the right, and how dare anyone challenge him?

"Let's listen," I told the executive.

"It doesn't matter if we listen," the executive said. "I'm right."

The executive was the boss, so the plant removed the older machines. The factory's performance promptly cratered. The team lead was right; we needed those older, faster machines to make enough tires to fill our orders. Without them, we were 6,000 tires a day short of our requirements.

The business center manager explained the problem and solution to me, and I overrode the executive and asked him to reinstall the old machines. That 6,000 gap in tire output vanished, and the cost to produce a tire also dropped by more than $2 per unit. We produced 12 million tires that year, so those savings had a $24 million effect on the bottom line.

Later on, the executive asked me how I knew what to do. "Simple," I told him. "I listened to the expert."

Like many leaders, the executive was happy to stay in his comfort zone, where he was a self-proclaimed expert. But this meant that his ego got in the way of doing what was best, and his pride paralyzed him—and, as a result, his organization. As Ellis Jones, a close friend as well as vice president and chief sustainability officer for global Goodyear, likes to say, "Every encounter matters." Have the humility to learn something. Don't be a snob, so consumed with your prejudices about the source that you overlook the solution. If the janitor has the best idea, use it!

That was frequently the situation I found myself in in Fayetteville. With an encyclopedic knowledge of the hidden factory, Sammy the janitor was a valuable ally. When replacement parts weren't on the shelves where they were supposed to be, Sammy knew where to find them. I learned to talk with Sammy before I held a town hall meeting, as Sammy could steer me right when my first instinct about how to frame a statement was wrong.

Because he was an expert in the plant's culture, Sammy was the equivalent of a native guide, able to steer me safely around danger. He was my champion, and his insights were my secret weapon. I think Sammy would have been happy to help other executives, but none of them had ever asked him.

Not listening to sources that they consider beneath them is just one of the mistakes executives commonly make. Top management often wants to improve business performance quickly. Shareholders and the board of directors want to see action, so the managers in charge of setting a new strategy come up with one or two plausible ideas—then they stop. They don't take the time they would need to dig into issues, so their ideas aren't as broad, systemic, or organic as they would need to be to create lasting change. These executives care too much about an idea's source and too little about whether the idea is a good solution to address a particular concern.

Their ideas also don't take the hidden factory into account because they don't see the hidden factory or take the time to talk with anyone who does. Developing relationships of trust with hourly workers takes time; people simply aren't going to tell you where the bodies are buried unless and until they trust that you aren't going to add your informants to the pile of corpses.

UNBIASED EXCELLENCE

In many organizations, women and people of color find that their opinions are less valued than those of their fair-skinned, male coworkers. This is comparable to the janitor or warehouse clerk whose ideas are not valued or solicited. Diversity in service of winning isn't only about valuing opinions of employees from all races and ethenicities or female points of view, or about considering the opinions of people in lower-tiered jobs. It's about valuing every point of view and bringing people together to share ideas.

Diversity, which considers *who* drives change, and inclusion, which considers *what* drives change, is about ownership. It's bigger than race, gender, or ethnic origin, or titles and rank within the organization. Embracing differences and seeing new perspectives and valuing job improvement proposals helps people and organizations grow. It fuels creativity and lets you anticipate and solve more problems. By getting input from a wide variety of people, you get that many more brains, eyes, and sets of life experience. This is the innovation engine of an organization.

Diversity in personal relationships also drives employees' feelings of investment in their jobs. It's relatively easy to quit early or decide against putting in extra effort when you don't know the other people who might be affected by your decision. But if you know that your lunch buddy Diane from another department needs your work product so she can do her own job, you are much more likely to stay a little late to get her the things she needs. When you understand that your friend will look at your work and know that it came from you, you might put a little more attention into making sure you're sending a high-quality product, because you care about your friend's good opinion.

When I first came to Fayetteville, the plant had an employee group called Justice for All, headed by three Black men. They'd take their requests to the human resources team. I sat in on one of the meetings and then told them that this was the last meeting we'd have in the current format.

Why? The group had no women, no Asians, no Hispanics. To me, that's not diversity. Later, the group came back to me and said, "We get it. You're not ignoring our platform. You're expanding it."

The lunchroom was self-segregated as well. Black employees sat together at one table, Asian workers at another, and Hispanic people at a third. People with every different kind of background worked together, but at mealtime, peer pressure kept them separate. The atmosphere reminded me of junior high. The few women in the plant were wildly talented, but no one seemed to notice their abilities.

When I came to the Fayetteville plant, I implemented the Billy Taylor six feet rule that I mentioned in Chapter 3: If you are within six feet of me, I'm going to say hello to you. I wanted to set a new norm: in this company and at this plant, we notice our colleagues. We interact with the people around us. I spent 80 percent of my time on the factory floor, walking around. I wanted to see how things were done, of course, but my bigger goal was to make myself accessible to everyone.

Telling me, "If you listen to them, they will listen to you," my janitor friend Sammy wisely suggested that I begin having lunch with five people a day, chosen from different groups around the factory that didn't already work together. I started with a disarming question, asking them to tell me their names, what they did, and one thing they're proud of in any part of their lives. Then I told them how the plant was doing overall and asked them to tell me what they saw working and not working. I also used this forum as a place to be deliberately clear about the successes, issues, and constraints the plant was experiencing. I never missed an opportunity to celebrate wins and discuss opportunities and current events.

The atmosphere in the factory changed almost immediately following this process. The meetings—and especially the question about what each participant was proud of—helped the walls come down. When one person said he was proud of his grandbaby, other participants remembered that and asked about the grandbaby. People stopped thinking of that man solely as "the Hispanic guy" and began thinking of him as "the proud grandfather." Relationships began to form from these informal conversations.

During breaks and lunch, employees stopped segregating themselves by ethnic background and started sitting with the people they worked with. It became socially acceptable to hang out with the people they wanted to be around.

This is a healthier way to live and a better way to grow the organization. It's also the only way an organization can engage people in sharing insights between functions. Ideas can come from anyone, as long as we create a place for those ideas to surface. To do that, you need to focus on the workers and how you can include them in a culture that normalizes sharing ideas.

Any one of us might have a good idea or efficient practice that would help another person work better. But unless we know and respect each other's contribution and value proposition, that insight stays inside a very small group. Migrating those insights to a bigger platform helps the manager drive change. As I mentioned earlier, there's no such thing as a manager who knows the ins and outs of everything that goes on in a business. Good ideas have a much better shot at spreading when working people talk to each other. During my keynotes, I tell the audience that the key to my success in my leadership is that I'm smart enough to get 13 degrees. I earned two of them and I hired 11. I use all of them daily to drive my success.

> Ideas can come from anyone, as long as we create a place for those ideas to surface.

BUILDING PROCESS EVANGELISTS

Just as I enforce the same standards for everyone, I'll take a good idea from anywhere. I didn't come to Goodyear with plans to change the culture from the top. I looked for the best ideas from all over, from the janitor on up. You can't just get all your ideas from an inner circle; you have to include everyone.

Human beings want to be valued. It's a need that's embedded in our souls. I greet people and remember their names; I'm excited to see them. I believe in noticing where people are capable of growth, setting them up for success, and celebrating their wins. Make people visible, and they'll make you valuable.

I saw enterprise evangelism in action when I visited Autoliv, an Ogden, Utah, company that makes automobile safety supplies using lean manufacturing principles. Its leaders did transformation *with* the people, not *to* the people, connecting people, processes, and tools into an ecosystem. Their workers were evangelists for their work process. Whenever a new employee started, the process evangelist led the way.

> **Make people visible, and they'll make you valuable.**

Many companies let the people at the top make all the decisions. Autoliv turns that upside down. On the tour I took, the hourly workers explained the business. They had work standards and specifications: the recipes they used to get work done. Aligning to win means having the right people doing the right jobs with the right tools, the right way. They know what they own and what they should be doing, and they become experts at their jobs.

THE BUCK STOPS WITH YOU

We've talked about how you can build an organizational culture, a viral system of extreme ownership that can and should outlast your time at the organization. That's true—and at the same time, your role in this system is vital. After all, you are in charge of everything, and the entire enterprise rests on your shoulders.

You aren't the person who handles every job in your business, the guy who makes the tires, cleans the bathroom, sends out the press releases, maintains the machines, hires and fires, and negotiates contracts with clients and suppliers. That would (most likely) be physically impossible, and in any case it's not how this system works. You're in charge of leading your team to victory.

Even when a team is motivated to succeed and clear on what success means, having the right leader at the helm is crucially important. In their book *Extreme Ownership: How U.S. Navy Seals Lead and Win*, former SEALs Jocko Willink and Leif Babin describe a training protocol for hopeful SEALs. Running on multiple nights of sleep deprivation, six teams of trainees raced each other up and down a beach at night. They had to run down the beach while carrying a heavy rubber dinghy, get into the water, capsize their boat so that every trainee was in the ocean, right the boat, get everyone back in, and then row like mad to be the first team across a finish line. The winning team got to rest during the next set of exercises, a much-appreciated prize for competitors who hadn't slept in three days.

On the day Willink and Babin describe, team two was consistently winning and team six was always the loser. Team two did get a boost from the rest time they earned, but it was also clear that its members worked like a well-oiled machine. The exercise instructors of course hassled team six and its leader about coming in last every time. The team leader responded by berating the team's members, shouting criticism and abuse.

Team six's leader protested. His team's poor performance wasn't his fault, he said. It wasn't a matter of leadership. He was trying to lead a team of incompetent soldiers. Despite his best efforts, team six just didn't have what it took to win.

Okay, the instructors said. Let's try an experiment. They swapped the two groups' leaders, so that now team six's leader was in charge of top-performing team two, and team two's leader was in charge of team six, the team that had consistently come in last. Team two's captain didn't look thrilled, but he didn't have a lot of choice in the matter. Team six's captain was thrilled. At last, he would have a competent team to command.

The teams raced down the beach. In the last hundred yards, team six drew even with team two, then slowly pulled ahead. The forever-last team had finally won. Though team two gave team six a run for its money, team six won every race for the rest of the night, with team two coming in second. Team two was full of solid individual performers. Under their first captain, they'd learned to work as a team. That skill didn't abandon them when their initial leader went to another team.

Team six saw a far bigger change. Its members went from having a leader who thought they couldn't win to having a leader who was quite certain that they could and would win. That made all the difference.

Assuming that everyone has the same basic competency, there are no bad teams—only bad leaders. You need to believe that your team can win. Your team needs both your belief and your guidance as they work toward winning. If you or another leader in your organization simply can't or won't believe that winning is possible, that person needs to step aside. Positive leadership is that important.

If someone on your team isn't winning, that person probably isn't incompetent and most likely isn't out to get you. It's much more likely that your team member doesn't understand one or more aspects of the overall strategy and how their individual efforts contribute to that strategy Or, that person doesn't have everything necessary to properly complete the key performance actions. In other words, when you have the option of blaming someone else, assume instead that the problem is you. Your leadership is vital to your organization's success.

CONSIDER THIS

As you finish this chapter, consider:

- How can you foster ownership rather than accountability?
- What strategies can you use to increase diversity and encourage social mixing within your workforce?
- Is your workplace highly stratified, with some people enjoying much higher status than others?
- How can you ask all your employees for ideas and insights?
- What might make it feel safer for employees to respond honestly?

CHAPTER 5

Executing Winning

At this point in our journey, you have learned to create a strategy and clearly communicate what that strategy means to everyone in your organization.

We have talked about committing to excellence by defining winning and aligning and deploying the strategy for extreme ownership. Now, we will focus on executing the strategy. For that equation—strategy plus execution—to equal winning, the strategy and mindset behind it must go viral throughout the organization. At an organization that has more than a few employees, the leader can't be the person who checks that everyone is executing the strategy and looks for ways to improve it. It's simply not possible to have enough direct time with everyone.

Even if your group only has a few members, you still don't want to be the person who micromanages the strategy and its execution. At its core, operational excellence is about problem solving and constraint elimination. You want a smooth, continuous flow of product and information.

Execution means doing the work of turning strategy into results. It means consistently looking for better ways to approach each task, as well as working to solve problems through eliminating waste in people, processes, and assets. When everyone in your organization is looking for efficiencies and ways to solve problems, you go from having one brain—yours—to having as many brains as you have people.

PERFORMANCE MAPPING

To build the strategy, we used purpose mapping. To deploy the strategy, we used ownership mapping. To deliver results, we will use performance mapping, connecting the critical performance indicator to every operation in the strategy. Performance mapping is a combination of *value stream mapping* and *process mapping*.

The value stream map displays all the steps our work process requires to deliver the critical performance indicator, from start to finish. This lets us visualize every task in the process and create single-glance status reports about each area's progress. The process map is a planning and management tool that visually displays the workflow from start to finish. Figure 5.1 shows a typical value stream map.

We use both because the value stream map looks at work across the organization, including functions, tiers, and processes. The process map looks at work within a process, function, or department, as well as considering the steps that go into completing an individual task. Every employee has key actions, metrics, and goals. The expectations for every worker track back to the organization's overarching goal. At Goodyear, that's the strategic plan for the North American division.

The strategy deployment model drives goal-setting and performance tracking *downward*. Instead of asking

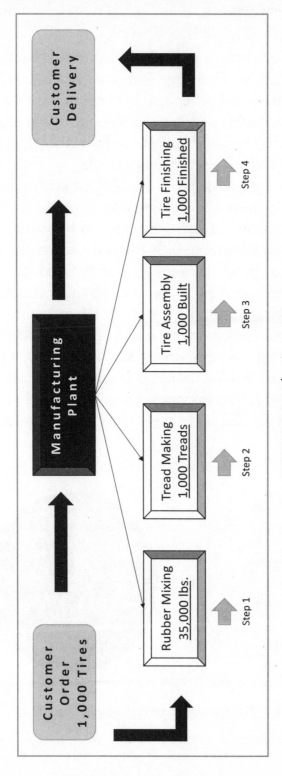

FIGURE 5.1 Value Stream Map

each associate to set goals based on what they think they can accomplish, we challenge each associate by asking them to work toward goals we give them to collectively make our plant and our company successful. Our team focuses on what we can do to get results, rather than on what we want to do to get through the day.

The concept of 8-4-2-1 supports performance mapping. Starting at the top, we break down each organizational goal into objectives assigned to the next level down (Figures 5.2 and 5.3). If the plant manager has $8 million to spend, then the production and quality managers can spend no more than $8 million collectively, so they get $4 million each. The four managers at the next level down can spend no more than $8 million collectively, so they each get $2 million, and so on. The practice of 8-4-2-1 cascades down every chain of command and across every level to make sure that all individual goals add up to meet the overall organization's goals.

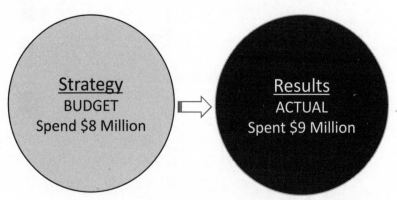

The plant overspent by $1 Million. What should we focus on to address the gap in performance?

FIGURE 5.2 Performance Mapping Organizational Goal

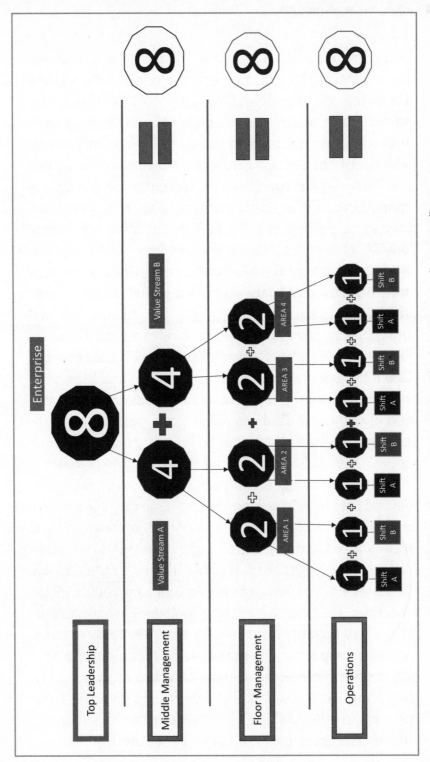

Enterprise

Top Leadership

Middle Management

Floor Management

Operations

Value Stream A

Value Stream B

AREA 1 AREA 2 AREA 3 AREA 4

Shift A Shift B Shift A Shift B Shift A Shift B Shift A Shift B

FIGURE 5.3 Performance Mapping Breaks the Larger Goal into Smaller Targets

By breaking the targets into smaller goals, you can track constraints that prevent the organization from achieving its overall goal (Figure 5.4). Without the performance mapping process, if we budgeted $8 million but spent $9 million instead, we wouldn't know who spent the extra $1 million. We'd order the whole company to stop spending: no traveling, no hiring, no consultants. We used this umbrella approach because we had no process to tell us where the issue was. With 8-4-2-1, the issue's location was obvious.

In the past, to tell workers about goals and performance standards, managers filled visual management and communications boards with the information we thought our associates needed. We expected them to have the time and interest to stop and read those boards. Often the boards contained many charts and lists, presented in a visually complex way that was hard to digest quickly. Those boards enabled poor performance. If employees weren't interested in knowing how they were doing, they could easily ignore them.

The power of 8-4-2-1 performance mapping goes beyond setting goals. It breaks larger, abstract goals into reasonable, concrete goals for every worker (Figure 5.5). If the whole factory needs to make eight tires (a simplification, of course), then each of two divisions should make four tires. Each of two areas in every division should make two tires. Every area has two employees, which means that every employee must make one tire. Because most of our people want to contribute in meaningful ways, job-specific goals let them know how they can personally help the plant succeed. It also shows company leaders the performance flow, which helps them successfully manage the intersections and create continuous product flow.

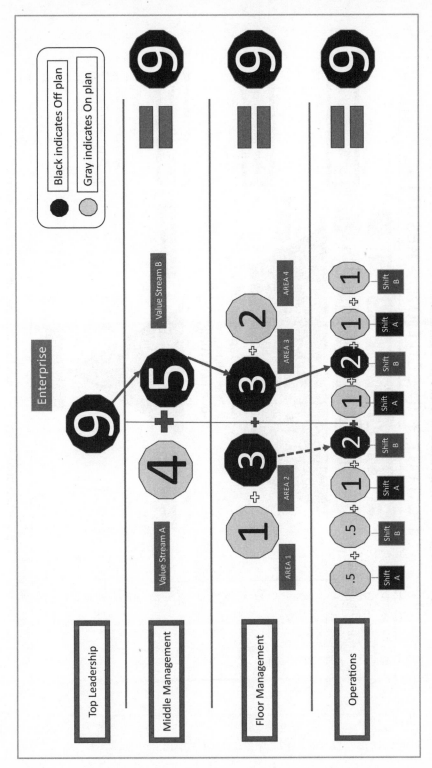

FIGURE 5.4 Performance Tracking

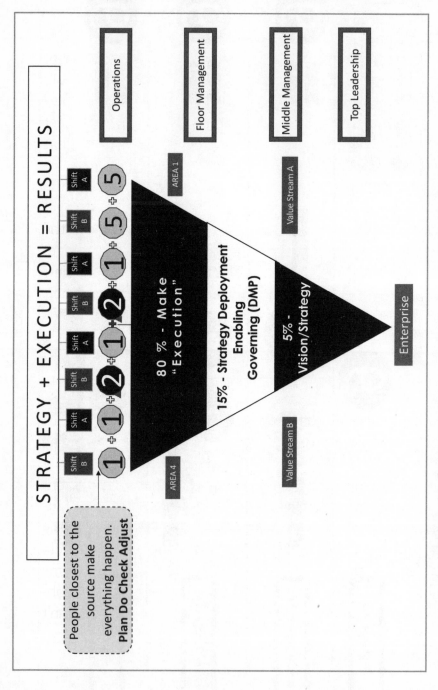

FIGURE 5.5 Performance Mapping Leads to Concrete Goals for Every Worker

THE DAILY MANAGEMENT SYSTEM

Imagine that you're a playwright. You've written a script and hired actors for each role in that script. The actors have learned their parts, and you're ready to begin performances. You still need the whole company to meet before and after each performance to talk about what went well, what wasn't so great, and how you can solve problems and remove constraints. Those two huddle review processes are key to an effective daily management system and to managing the intersections of the functions and tiers of the enterprise. Daily management systems (DMS) are a set of management review processes through which team members evaluate their progress toward accomplishing the company's strategic objectives.

You can't just build a strategy, explain individual roles in that strategy to everyone in the organization, shout "Go!" and assume that flawless execution will follow. You need a daily management system that lets your company support and lead its people as they turn the strategy into action and action into results. The daily management process should also create an environment where hiding problems is unacceptable. The daily management system advocates for transparently exposing problems, effectively solving them, and asking for help (and getting it) whenever necessary to solve problems and eliminate constraints. If you're in business, problems will surface constantly. When enterprises don't understand and solve those problems, there will be negative consequences.

A daily management system gives managers, teams, and individuals at every level of the company the structure they need to link performance actions to metrics and goals. It gives them a structured way to capture anything that's going wrong or constraining the organization from meeting its objectives, ideally before a problem has the chance to grow into an emergency.

WHAT A DAILY MANAGEMENT SYSTEM ISN'T

A daily management system (DMS) isn't an opportunity to show off stable production, operational efficiency, or data collected over a week, month, or year, although it's important to recognize successes and accomplishments. You don't need to create a PowerPoint presentation for a daily management meeting. Rather, daily management system meetings are places for teams to identify opportunities, understand root causes of issues, track improvements, and bring chaotic situations under control. Key performance indicators marked with green dots probably don't need discussion during DMS meetings. This is a place to intervene in the KPIs that are marked red.

DMS meetings ultimately fuel a culture of continuous improvement. Continuous improvement isn't possible if the job is left to just a few process improvement experts who work for senior management. It's only possible if team members across the organization at all levels regularly check their progress relative to their goals and take corrective action when they spot problems. Continuous improvement starts at the shop floor, where individuals and work groups do the value-added labor.

SOLVING DMS CHALLENGES

As with any new behavior, DMS has an adaptation phase as managers and employees start transparently exposing their work-system failures. This requires the blame-free lean culture to be functional in every work area so that the work team can focus on improving KPIs that are in the red.

Strong managers who engage their employees and are proficient in team-based approaches to improvement adapt to DMS as an immediate problem-solving tool quicker than those who prefer the comfort of offering mostly "green day" metrics. These strong managers are more likely to move the goalposts by choosing new metrics throughout the year as previous problems are resolved. Many will adopt a rule that three months of all green days signals problem resolution and stability. They can retire the current metric.

Work systems that do their jobs in a structure of serial handoffs connected along the workflow path should consider displaying all of their visual metric boards in the same place. That helps them work together more readily and quickly spot connections between their metrics, as well as any glitches in those connections.

HOW TO EFFECTIVELY RUN A DMS MEETING

Keep it brief. You should conduct the meeting standing up, which encourages brevity. You can note green metrics, but don't discuss them. You are there for a visual review of the daily management board, quickly documenting and assessing any breakdowns in key processes within the previous 24 hours. In my experience, a DMS meeting takes perhaps 10 to 15 minutes for each daily management board. You'll find that you spend more time when you're dealing with more problems and less time when things are going well.

A leader might also want to spend additional time talking with workers by segueing from a DMS meeting to a Gemba walk, which is the lean manufacturing process of walking around the work floor, seeing the actual process, to understand the work being done, and ask questions of the person doing the work, enabling the worker and learning from the experience. The goal of the Gemba walk is to understand the workplace and its constraints, rather than focus on results. A Gemba walk is not a place to play "gotcha," or an opportunity to point out faults, play boss, or force a personal agenda. It's a way to gather information.

In lean management culture, leaders support improvement processes by managing the intersections between people, process, and assets. Leaders engage, empower, and coach the team through the improvement process, all without taking over. The answers lie with those doing the work, and the leader who recognizes this develops the workers' abilities and reinforces this approach to solving problems.

CALIBRATING THE MANAGEMENT SYSTEM

You already know that you'll need to be clear in how you define winning, and you have performance mapped what your people own. You will also need to be extremely clear about the key performance actions you hope will help your team win.

It can be challenging for a team to stick to key performance actions as a workday, week, or month unfolds. Problems crop up, and ongoing situations are often fluid. Employees need to talk with each other about how things are going, discuss problems, and brainstorm solutions as their work progresses. This way, you can catch problems midstream when potential solutions may be clearest, as well as after the fact when you have the option of making systemwide changes. In doing so, you have an opportunity to create a continuous improvement process.

PLAN, DO, CHECK, ADJUST

To control and continuously improve processes, products, and results, I use the plan, do, check, adjust method (PDCA). PDCA is also called the Deming cycle, Shewhart cycle, control cycle, or plan-do-study-act (PDSA). We incorporated PDCA into our daily management process.

At Goodyear, I found that the best system for using key performance actions to solve problems was this:

1. **Plan.** We began by hypothesizing which actions would be helpful. What key performance actions do you believe will help the organization win? Take your hypothesis to the individual level. Talk to workers and their managers. What does each person need to do to meet their own goals? How will those individual goals contribute to meeting the organization's larger goals?

2. **Do.** Track performance as individuals and teams follow through on the plan.

3. **Check.** Verify that people followed your organization's standard methods for getting things done. Test the new hypothesis. What are the results? Did things go the way you thought they would? What surprises cropped up? What constraints and problems needed solving?

4. **Adjust.** Be agile. The only constant in business is change. You need to solve the problems at the source and adjust so that you can resolve constraints and prevent abnormalities. Be prepared for surprises. You should change anything about the plan or process that didn't contribute to individual and organizational success.

Everyone in your company should learn to repeat this four-part process over and over, every day, every week, and every month, through a daily management process. Plan your work for the day, then follow through on the plan. Check whether your plan is contributing to winning as you've defined it. Make the adjustments, solving problems and eliminating constraints so that the plan contributes to individual and group goals.

To make sure that this process was running as we intended at the Goodyear plant, we put multiple management meetings in place. We used these meetings to manage the intersections, because a process had representation from multiple functions:

- Every month, each shift had an operating review.

- Every week, each function within the plant had an operating review.
- Every day, each tier had an operating review.
- Every hour, individual workers met with their shift supervisors.

Even this plan, which is already quite spelled out, benefits from deliberate clarity, as I learned when I was in charge of Goodyear's plant in Fayetteville, North Carolina. We had a morning meeting, then dismissed the attendees to execute that strategy. I was full of optimism. Then we missed our performance goal—yet again.

Why did we miss? We didn't start by considering the reasons behind both the meeting and the performance goal. We had no leadership standards that focused on the purpose of the meeting, how the meeting should be run, and the desired deliverables. We were the problem, but we blamed the people when we failed.

Factory leaders weren't entirely clear about how the meeting schedule linked to the overall enterprise strategy. As a result, workers were doing what leaders told them to do. We'd told workers to meet every two hours. Ever obedient, they met every two hours. We should have told them to use those meetings to PDCA, to discuss how their work was progressing versus the target, identify any issues they were having, and brainstorm what they would do to solve those issues. Unfortunately, because we didn't tell them what those meetings were for, they didn't use the time as we had planned. Deliberate clarity wasn't engrained in the culture. The purpose and deliverables for the meeting were not clear, so we were trying to manage a secret.

There's a big difference between a culture in which
the workers do what the bosses tell them to do—nothing
more, nothing less—and one in which workers are genuinely invested in reaching their own goals and the
facility's goals. If you're doing what I tell you, you'll meet
with other workers every two hours and discuss whatever you feel like talking about: the weather, the local
sports teams, what you've brought for lunch. (I freely
admit that was on me; I should have been much more
specific.) The absence of ownership results in blame. We
were blaming the frontline leaders at the plant for what
wasn't their fault.

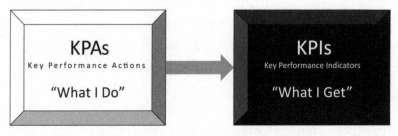

FIGURE 5.6 Converting KPAs to KPIs

Throughout this process, we convert strategy to
action, and then action to results (Figure 5.6). An
individual performs every action; improvements then
happen because those individual workers practice the
individual job components that, taken together, move
the key performance indicators. Workers convert actions
into results. They take ownership of those actions, and
in doing so, they are no longer cogs in a machine without interest in how the things they do contribute to the
company's success or failure.

Scorecards are filled with KPIs. These are lagging indicators. KPAs, key performance actions, are leading indicators; moreover, they are the actions that deliver the results. Figure 5.7 compares the various aspects of key performance actions and key performance indicators.

	Key Performance Actions (KPAs)	Key Performance Indicators (KPIs)
Results	Behavior or Actions	Measurements
Focus	Proactive	Reactive
Accountability	Assigned Individual Accountability to Drive Ownership	Assigned Team Accountability of Measurements
Improvement	People Up	Top Down
Feedback	Individual Action Register to Eliminate Constraints	Team Scorecard
Mindset	What Actions to Take to Improve the Measurement.	Are We Winning or Losing
Indicator	Leading (Before and During)	Lagging (After)
Summary	Actions Drive Team Performance	We Measure Team Performance

FIGURE 5.7 Comparing Key Performance Actions and Key Performance Indicators

Every key performance action is performed by an individual, and improvements happen because individual workers practice the actions that, taken together, move the key performance indicators. When you break down individual job components, workers can see additional actions they could take that would improve performance even more.

They take ownership of those actions and they're no longer cogs in a machine, subject to the whims of

> Individual workers are genuine CEOs of the portion of the business that stands before them, and they can see how regular, consistent effort creates measurable change.

people above them and with no real interest in how the things they do contribute to the company's success or failure. Individual workers are genuine CEOs of the portion of the business that stands before them, and they can see how regular, consistent effort creates measurable change.

Give people the support they need to do new things well, including time to learn and practice, and avoid blame. Individual blame leads to hesitation, withdrawal, and holding back—exactly the behavior that we want to reduce as we move people toward feeling more engaged, empowered, and responsible.

You may remember my weight-loss example from Chapter 2. As a reminder, here it is again. My crucial performance indicator is my weight. I hope to lose 50 pounds in 25 weeks. Here, we revisit the example, applying what we've learned thus far (Figure 5.8).

My Planned Actions: KPAs
- Eat 2,500 calories a day
- Each week eat chocolate no more than once
- Each week eat pizza or pasta no more than once
- Drink no more than two glasses of wine per week
- Walk two miles a day
- Sleep at least seven hours each night

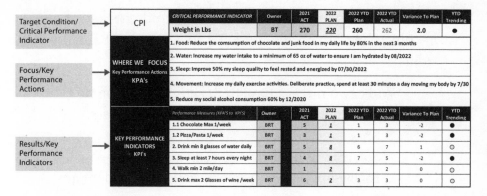

FIGURE 5.8 Weight Loss KPAs and KPIs—Purpose Map

I can measure each one of these KPAs as a KPI.

My Performance: KPIs
- Eat a maximum of 2,500 calories a day: Green/ Achieved target
- Each week eat chocolate no more than once: Green/Achieved target
- Each week eat pizza or pasta no more than once: Green/Achieved target
- Drink no more than two glasses of wine: Green/ Achieved target
- Walk two miles a day: Red/Did not achieve target
- Sleep at least seven hours each night: Green/ Achieved target

My CPI (Critical Performance Indictor)
- I lost 30 pounds in six months. This is progress, but it means that I missed my goal by 20 pounds.

I made a plan, executed my plan, and checked the results. Now I examine my KPIs to see where I should adjust.

- Walk two miles a day: Red/Did not achieve target
  - **Root cause:** Shoes hurt feet, caused blisters. Shoes too small.
  - **Solution:** Bought new shoes.
  - **Follow-up:** Blisters healed. Walking without pain.

I can now hypothesize that what kept me from meeting my goal was missing out on my daily two-mile walk. With new shoes on my feet, I can try again to lose that remaining 20 pounds by being more consistent with that KPA.

VISUAL MANAGEMENT'S 10-SECOND RULE

Executing winning requires knowing the score. At any given time, the people doing the work need to know if they are winning or losing. The information should be highly visible and easy to translate and trigger a call to action. The problem with most companies that I work with as an operating system architect is that their score-boards are scorecards reside in managers' computers. There's nothing wrong with keeping track of score-cards in a computer, and in general that's where I think managers should keep track of scorecards for an entire organization. For executives, I like a high-tech, low-touch approach to following key performance actions and indicators.

For the people actually doing the work, however, I like exactly the opposite: low-tech and high touch. Scorecards need to be where workers can see them. When you drive by a billboard, you quickly understand and retain the information you see. Scorecards should act like billboards, informing workers whether they are winning or losing. In fact, the visual management boards need to be where workers cannot easily avoid seeing them. If you want doctors to wash their hands before they see patients, for example, you can't hide information about how well the handwashing campaign is going in an administrator's computer. You need a big scorecard board at the central office, nurse's station, break room, or anywhere else physicians congregate.

> For executives, I like a high-tech, low-touch approach to following key performance actions and indicators. For the people actually doing the work, however, I like exactly the opposite: low-tech and high touch.

THE IMPACT OF KNOW AND HOW IT DRIVES PERFORMANCE

Visual management boards provide status at a glance, displaying current performance in relation to target performance. An effective visual management board contains three elements: performance standards, actual performance in relation to the standard, and problems/actions taken to solve problems.

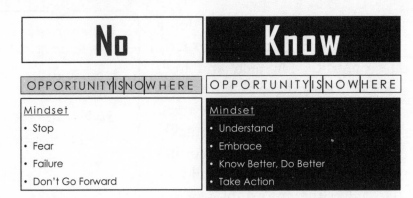

FIGURE 5.9 How Our Mindset Can Change When We Know

Visual boards provide clarity, like a scoreboard at a football or basketball game (Figure 5.9). They highlight the current reality—the score—and let you compare it against the target reality, which probably involves your team winning the game. With the scoreboard out of sight, people lose track of what they're trying to achieve. A scoreboard reminds you of your goals and your status with respect to those goals in 10 seconds or less. Scoreboards are a closed-loop system that makes your work, your progress, and the ongoing commitment to your responsibility easily visible.

We focus on the things we measure, and our focus should be on our goals. Visual management creates a level of awareness and motivates people to take action. It encourages ownership and highlights any gap between the current reality and the goal. Boards are self-explanatory and easy to understand at a glance.

In Fayetteville, individuals' mission-critical goals were posted on red/green boards at the workstation. Red/green boards are a critical tool for engaging workers. To use the board, they must know and understand their key metrics and how to measure their own performance.

They also have to physically flip the tag to show red if they are failing and green if they are succeeding. This physical and personal interaction with their metrics drives workers to succeed. When they see that they are in the red midway through the day, they push themselves to be in the green by the end of the shift. Because we placed the responsibility and control for performance in the hands of the true experts—the people who do the job—we created a plant full of plant managers. Every associate is the plant manager for his workstation.

The other advantage of red/green boards is that the information on them can be interpreted in 10 seconds or less. Within 10 seconds, anyone can see whether the process is performing to plan, and if not, where the issue is. The combination of engaged associates and 10-second performance evaluation lets our management team spend more time coaching and addressing poor performers and less time digging through stacks of reports.

It also eliminates the practice of addressing poor performance with a "peanut-butter spread" approach. Instead of lecturing the entire team about performance problems, we address only the individuals with performance issues. For example, our board meetings used to last longer than 40 minutes, and everyone felt chastised when performance was poor. Now they only last 5 to 10 minutes and we focus on areas that are not meeting their goals.

MEASURE WHAT MATTERS

The information on a scorecard should be simple and relevant to the people who are looking at it. In a hospital setting where the goal is to reduce the number of hospital-acquired infections in surgical patients, you might post a scorecard that lists just two numbers: the number of surgeries to date and the number of hospital-acquired infections in those surgical patients. That's what matters, and that's what the people on the front line need to know.

A manager will probably track multiple scorecards, and those scorecards may include additional information that the workforce doesn't need. It's not that this information is kept secret, it's just that it would over-complicate a workforce scorecard. As I decided when I looked at communications boards at Fayetteville, if you can't understand a scorecard in 10 seconds or less, that scorecard is too complicated. Make visual management meaningful to the people who are looking at it. What you post should help workers make decisions. It should tell them where to focus.

For instance, maybe you'd like to prevent hospital-acquired infections by encouraging physicians, nurses, and other patient-facing caregivers to wash their hands and cover their sneezes. As a manager, you might also be tracking not just the number of surgeries and hospital-acquired infections, but also which surgeons performed those surgeries, which floors of the hospital housed patients with infections, and which antibiotics were or were not effective in combating those infections. That's too much information for a worker-focused scorecard. It gives the medical personnel information that they can't directly affect. Don't gum up the works with data that's superfluous to the people who are looking at it.

As I said, it's fine—even required, most of the time—for a manager to track more than one scorecard. It's also a good practice for workers to develop their own, individual scorecards. If I'm a physician working to reduce infectious disease, maybe my scorecard would let me mark my patient interactions and whether I washed my hands on the way into each one of them. My weight-loss project would benefit from a daily journal in which I write down what I eat, how much I eat, and how much I exercise.

Fit the scorecard to the people who will look at it. Give them the crucial information they can digest in 10 seconds or less, and store other information elsewhere.

CELEBRATE THE RED

As I said, red status on a management board helps motivate people to do what they need to do to get into the green. At the same time, it's important not to punish people when key performance indicators are in the red.

Red status is like a definite diagnosis from your physician. Of course, you aren't going to be happy that you're sick, but now you know what's wrong. Once you have that diagnosis, your physician probably has ideas about what can be done to fix the problem.

> **Red status is like a definite diagnosis from your physician.**

When a status board has a red dot, that's something to celebrate. Instead of knowing that something, somewhere in your operation is keeping it from reaching its critical goals, you know exactly what isn't running according to plan and where that problem or constraint is occurring. The system has told you what's wrong and where the failure point is. Now you know what needs fixing.

CONSIDER THIS

As you conclude this chapter, consider:

- Does your scorecard tell you if you are winning or losing in 10 seconds or less and from 10 feet away?
- What is your current performance status?

CHAPTER 6

Building a Culture of Continuous Improvement

There is no finish line.

You can't be the only person driving positive change in your organization; there's only one you. There are many other change agents in your workforce. For continuous improvement to genuinely catch on, you need other people to practice, notice ways to improve, set goals, and show other workers what they're doing.

By successfully evangelizing your workforce, you outsource your problems to a wider set of strengths and idea sources than you could ever muster on your own. Sometimes people feel threatened when they discover that employees who are under them in an organizational chart are smart and capable. That's a mistake. Your company thrives when it enthusiastically accepts smart ideas from anyone who has them. Leaders should inspire people to be evangelists for how we get things done.

In Fayetteville, continuous improvement was led and owned by the people. Senior leadership's role was to enable, empower, and support. A continuous improvement manager and a team of continuous improvement specialists led the

> **By successfully evangelizing your workforce, you outsource your problems to a wider set of strengths and idea sources than you could ever muster on your own.**

effort. The mix of salaried and hourly associates effectively demonstrated an ability to analyze and think creatively and strategically. Because these employees were closest to the actual work, they analyzed performance in their areas and on their machines to identify and prioritize improvement needs. They facilitated their own continuous improvement projects.

We used three different approaches to pursue continuous improvement and reduce waste:

- **Formal continuous improvement projects.** These projects required a multifunctional team and took more than one week to accomplish.
- **Rapid improvement activities.** These projects required a multifunctional team and no more than one week to accomplish.
- **Work Simple projects, abbreviated as WorkSimp.** These ideas, which generally concerned simple solutions, could be accomplished by one to three associates and weren't limited to a set period of time. WorkSimps required associates to be involved and substantially responsible for completing work on their own ideas.

  Hourly workers, salaried workers, and even vendors were eligible to take part in WorkSimps. Any associate could have an idea and get that idea evaluated directly by a manager or by filling out a WorkSimp card. We minimized the effort we spent evaluating potential ideas by focusing on what workers needed to successfully implement their own ideas, then making sure those resources were available.

  Some projects didn't fill a concrete business need, but letting associates make changes, even irrelevant ones, stretched their ability to think outside the box. It encouraged them to take initiative and prepared them to help us find solutions to business-critical issues. It created continuous improvement evangelists.

When people know what they own, they have the autonomy to drive change. Just as I enforce the same standards for everyone, I'll take a good idea from anywhere. I didn't come to Goodyear with plans to change the culture from the top. I looked for the best ideas from all over, from the janitor on up. You need to include everyone. You can't just get all your ideas from an inner circle.

Leaders have to let go, but they don't have to let loose. Ensure that each member of an organization knows what she owns and has the tools she needs to do the job. Then let her do that job without micromanaging or managing people who are one or more levels below your direct reports. Check back with employees regularly to make sure they're on track for winning, providing whatever support they need to make that happen. Make sure the people you directly supervise do the same for employees who report to them.

> ⌒
> **Leaders have to let go, but they don't have to let loose.**

DELIBERATE PRACTICE AND SCIENTIFIC THINKING

It was important for us to teach employees the habits of deliberate practice and scientific thinking. It's easy to think of a factory job as mindless. I'm sure you'll find that's true of many jobs. You punch in, do a task over and over, and punch out again. Just another day, earning just another dollar. To continuously improve, your team needs to see their work as something that involves their mind.

Ownership is the core of winning through lean transformation, but ownership is just a shell without scientific thinkers (innovation) and deliberate practice. Getting good at a job is part of the process of continuous improvement. Once you've become as good as you can be within the bounds of an existing process, you are able to look for places to change that process so that you can more efficiently reach the same result.

Deliberate practice is practice that has the goal of improving overall performance by working hard to improve a smaller section of that performance. You aren't just repeating a task by rote. For example, a violinist spends a relatively small proportion of her practice time playing a piece all the way through. She spends much more time perfecting the parts that she finds difficult or tricky. She plays those sections slowly, and then up to speed.

Then she joins the rest of an orchestra or chamber group, which practices the same way. The group spends extra time on difficult passages, entrances, cues, and transitions. They practice solo and in smaller groups, working their way up to the full orchestra. An hour of a morning-long rehearsal might be spent with other first or second violinists, working out the kinks in that group's part of a symphony in a practice that's called a "sectional." With their parts learned, the sections combine to rehearse as a full orchestra. Much of the work is done individually, but the goal—the CPI—is to perform their best in concert.

Every time we practice a skill, solo or as a group, the goal is to figure out a procedure that consistently works in a variety of situations. A violinist gets a sense of how much rosin a bow should get and decides on the fingering she'll use for every part of a composition. A chamber music group decides who will cue the beginning of a new movement.

People who practice like this are using the scientific method. We start with a hypothesis: one hour of violin practice, twice a week, will improve your performance. During your sessions you break down every element of how you will play. You work on continuously improving each element. You document each step and what you changed to improve and incorporate those moves into your new operating standard. You continue to try to implement new ideas and try out other hypotheses. Eventually you arrive at an optimal performance standard and process: working out the fiddly bits like so, using this brand of strings, and working with that teacher equals the best, most consistent, highest-quality performance.

A violinist's process may be more individual than that of a factory worker. In either job, however, individuals can learn things that they pass along to their coworkers. Perhaps the violinist determines that a given fingering is the best way to play a piece of music. She shares that with everyone else in her section. They test that fingering, comparing it against other ways they've tried playing the same music. At the end of the process, everyone in the section is using the best, most efficient method.

Before you implement a new idea or solution, you should validate its impact (Figure 6.1). I call this going an inch wide and a mile deep. Prove it, challenge it, and trust it before you implement it across an organization. Then cascade improvements across multiple processes with a documented standard.

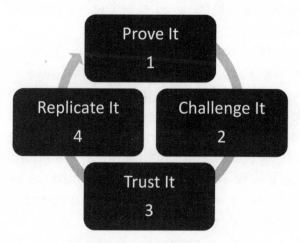

FIGURE 6.1 Validate the Solution:
Prove It, Challenge It, Trust It, Replicate It

When you've practiced enough to have a sense of what you should standardize, you should next focus on continuous improvement, using a four-step process. For example, McDonald's is a model of consistency and continuous improvement. It follows the prove, trust, challenge, and replicate model.

First, you prove that the standard you're proposing works. McDonald's has clearly devoted time and effort to demonstrating that its frozen potato sticks, submerged in oil that's at a consistent temperature for a set period of time, yield the same perfectly cooked fries every time.

Second, you need to challenge that standard. If two minutes at 500 degrees is good, is two minutes at 550 degrees better? What if we make the potato sticks thinner or thicker? Try out other logical possibilities to see if you can improve on your proposed standard.

Third, you must trust your results. If you have kept careful records of all your french fry experiments, you can rest assured that you are an expert, and that your recipe is *the* recipe.

Fourth, you are going to need to replicate your process and results. When McDonald's concluded that a combination of these specifically sized potato sticks, plus oil at that specific temperature, submerged for this many minutes, is the best possible combination, that combination became the standard for how every restaurant in the chain makes french fries. Variations from that process, such as the company's shift from cooking fries in beef tallow to using a combination of vegetable oil and beef flavoring, are deliberate. With nearly 40,000 locations worldwide, McDonald's doesn't believe in luck.

Goodyear doesn't believe in luck either. In a tire factory, we have new hires all the time, as well as established workers who are moving from one part of the operation to a function that's new to them. A person who is new to a job is trained and certified on every aspect of the job, including how to safely operate whatever machinery is involved. The training period can last up to six weeks and includes lots of practice to assure safety and quality, followed by quantity. Once a worker has learned a job's tasks and work standards, she is in a position to deliberately deliver a consistent product that exceeds customer expectations.

We also ask workers to deliberately look for ways to get better at their jobs. That includes individual performance. Ideally, we also hope that those improvements will go viral, as when I asked one worker with a well-organized workspace to give a talk to other workers about how to organize and clean their own workspaces. Once we plan, do, check, and adjust, we prove, trust, challenge, and replicate.

ROUTINE IS THE ENEMY OF GROWTH

Good is never good enough in business. Every organization needs to consistently improve standards and methods in its operation. That being said, it's critically important to know how and when to change them. Without ongoing assessments, practicing the way you always practice gets you the same results you've always gotten. If you always run four miles in one hour, continuing to run four miles in one hour is only going to get you the ability to run a mile in 15 minutes. No challenge, no change.

> ⬭
> **Don't let repetition desensitize you.**

If that's fine with you, carry on. But if you want continuous improvement, you'll have to shake things up. Don't let repetition desensitize you. Desensitization is what happens to people who live near a railroad track and eventually stop hearing the train, or who work at a perfume counter and eventually don't notice the scent. When we do the same things over and over again, we tend to run on autopilot. That gets in the way of focusing on improving the ways we do the sometimes-tedious tasks that provide organizational value.

Deliberate practice lets us blend tools, concepts, and techniques in new ways, consciously developing our skills through experimentation. It also lets us get the practice hours in that we need to become good at something. As the journalist Malcolm Gladwell asserted in his bestselling book *Outliers*, mastering an activity should take at least 10,000 hours of practice.

Deliberate practice has four core components—specific goals, intense focus, frequent discomfort, and immediate feedback (Figure 6.2)—that serve to force mental adaptation and innovative insight. Here is how deliberate practice works:

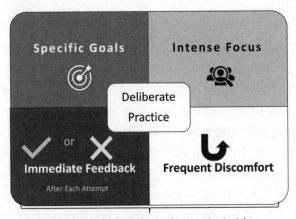

FIGURE 6.2 Core Components of Deliberate Practice

- **Talent alone isn't enough.** Talent is a fine starting point, and of course people can be more or less talented at (and interested in) a given task. But talent can only get you so far. To be really good at something, you need to practice. As it turns out, your piano teacher was right. The more you practice, the better you get.

- **Deliberate practice is more than simple repetition.** Doing something over and over won't necessarily help you develop a nuanced skill. To get better, you must both focus on the method you're using to do something and stretch yourself, trying to move a little faster, for instance, or reach a little farther (Figure 6.3). Eventually the new skills will become part of your muscle memory. It has been suggested that this takes an average of 66 days.

- **Break whatever you're practicing into manageable parts.** Don't try to play the whole sonata or skate the whole routine all at once—not at first, anyway. Practice small parts of the whole. Spend extra time on the parts you find difficult, or focus on where you think you have the greatest ability to improve.

- **Set goals and keep working toward them.** Maybe you can't run an eight-minute mile today; that's okay. Consistently work toward running a mile in eight minutes, persevering in trying different methods to run just a little faster during every practice session. Stretch outside your comfort zone.

- **Get real-time feedback.** Another set of eyes can be a huge help. Find a person who understands what you're trying to do and ask that person to watch you as you practice. Could he point out what you could do better? Does she have technique improvements to suggest? Document your results as you practice. Seeing your progress can be very motivating.

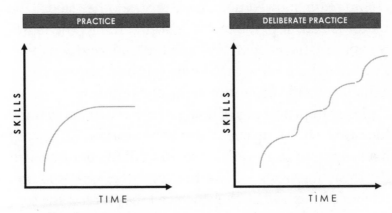

FIGURE 6.3 Ordinary Practice Versus Deliberate Practice

CELEBRATE THE PROCESS, EMBRACE THE INDIVIDUAL

Constructing a continuous improvement culture is a lot of work and may be a significant change from how things were previously done at your company. In Fayetteville, we needed a proactive culture where hourly workers were empowered to take corrective action against the root cause of problems to prevent those problems from cropping up again. At first, we had an arrangement where shift managers called senior managers before making a decision. An hourly operator had an issue with a machine and brought that issue to a manager's attention. Then, the shift manager called the senior leadership to ask for instructions or simply to report the news, sometimes at all hours of the day and night. That's a problem right there: the hourly operator didn't have the autonomy or power to fix the problem.

I recall being called to look at a piece of equipment that had a motor failure. The plant's entire senior leadership team showed up. One after the other said, "The motor is bad. Yep, the motor is bad." Finally, the maintenance manager said, "We need to replace the motor." Everyone there knew that. There was no reason to create a management convention to fix the problem.

Learning a new way of doing things wasn't always easy for Fayetteville employees. I wasn't surprised when they made some mistakes along the way. I didn't punish them for these mistakes—quite the contrary; I praised and celebrated them when they followed the process. The continuous improvement process naturally produces results, so teaching people to follow the process is of crucial importance. It's far more important than quibbling about whether or not they achieved ideal results right away.

As we continued building our continuous improvement process, we found that workers were increasingly enthusiastic about lean process management and were retaining what they had learned. Lean is the application of practices, principles, and tools to combat waste, eliminating anything that doesn't add value for the customer. Lean processes, tools, and ownership behaviors were starting to go viral as people shared what they'd learned.

To celebrate, we had a weekly continuous improvement review—otherwise known as "the best meeting of the week"—where people could show off their completed continuous improvement projects. Leadership teams gathered to watch and applaud as individuals and groups presented "before," "after," and their final results. A round of applause and handshakes followed every presentation.

Everyone who participated in a project got a certificate of accomplishment for following the process. Associates also got a bronze continuous improvement medal (Figure 6.4) and a continuous improvement T-shirt for their first project each year. Second projects merited a silver medal; third meant a gold medal. Anyone who took part in 12 or more projects in a calendar year got the coveted platinum medal and a continuous improvement racing jacket. Collecting those medals and race jackets drove good-natured competition and motivated employees to keep looking for the next project.

FIGURE 6.4 Recognition Medals

One might have expected strong resistance to change in a unionized plant like Fayetteville, but the opposite was the case. I have found that is often what happens when unions see that an underlying principle of lean manufacturing is to preserve jobs by increasing profitability, not to cut jobs to reduce costs.

Even for a union shop, Fayetteville enjoyed an unprecedented level of engagement and evangelism around lean management. In the beginning, when shop-floor workers presented their projects in twice-weekly meetings, we had average participation of about 38 people. During the first year, we averaged 262 participants a month; the second year saw an average of 532 participants.

Those 532 associates generated millions of dollars in savings. One month alone saw $1.8 million in savings from our plant. The evangelists were exposing the hidden factory: the things we walk by every day but have stopped seeing. With employees motivated to find improvements in their own processes, we continued to improve every day.

I saw this in action across an enterprise when I visited Autoliv, an Ogden, Utah, company that makes automobile safety supplies using lean manufacturing principles. They did transformation *with* the people, not *to* the people, connecting people, processes, and tools into an ecosystem. Because it was clear what roles people owned and what they needed to achieve, they became evangelists of how to get it done.

Many companies let the people at the top make all the decisions. Autoliv turns that upside down, as in our pyramid example. On the plant tour we took, the hourly workers explained the business and continuous improvement processes to the entire group. They had work standards and specifications: the recipes they used to get work done. Aligning to win means having the right people doing the right jobs with the right tools. They know what they own and what they should be doing, and they become experts at their jobs. Managers must trust the process. Let go. You don't have to let loose.

CUTTING COSTS WON'T CUT IT

It is important to note that cost cutting is not continuous improvement. Very often, management's top-down, full-speed approach is to cut costs. Cutting costs is a sure way to improve the bottom line, and it's typically very popular with top management. But this approach is not sustainable. You can't save your way to prosperity.

It's a mistake to make cutting costs your continuous improvement strategy. Building a continuous improvement culture is about effective problem solving and eliminating waste. Winning means finding (and implementing) the key performance actions and indicators that drive an organization's ability to fulfill its purpose. If that means spending less money on things that legitimately require less funding, that's great. But don't equate spending less money with winning. Your people may need the organization to spend money on continuous improvement projects in ways that help them do their jobs better, repaying the investment many times over.

> You can't save your way to prosperity.

For instance, I saw a situation in which a plant had gone over budget. The executives imposed a hiring freeze. No new jobs, no replacing employees lost to attrition. But the factory still kept going over budget. The reason, as it turned out, was that it had to pay workers overtime wages and hire contract labor at triple the usual pay rate to get through all its client orders. When they hired more workers, the plant was able to fill all its orders by paying regular wages. This move brought the whole operation back within the budget.

"Cutting costs" is frequently a euphemism for layoffs, as well as an expectation that people who still have jobs when the layoffs are over will now work harder, with fewer resources, to accomplish more. That's counterproductive in two ways. First, by eliminating jobs across the board, you're sending away the experts, the very people who could be telling you what they need to do their jobs more productively. Instead of listening, you've sent them to the unemployment line. There are certain business conditions that dictate the need to lay off workers, such as market share loss and business deterioration. But cutting jobs as a continuous improvement solution could be fatal to your continuous improvement journey.

Embracing change is a risk, but ignoring the need to change can destroy a business. Telling a manager—especially someone new, as I was at the time in Fayetteville—what resources you need to do your job more effectively is a risk. Learning new skills, or novel ways of practicing old skills, is a risk. Very few people are great at implementing new things right off the bat. People certainly don't voluntarily take those risks when they know they could lose their jobs at any time; instead, they keep their heads down and stay quiet. By embracing change and the people that do it, companies and leaders foster an environment of continuous improvement.

OPERATIONAL EXCELLENCE IS MORE THAN ITS TOOLS

Strategy, deliberate practice, problem solving, follow-through—they're all important. In the end, however, all of these things are tools. The best problem-solving method and process is the one your company commits to implementing.

When I arrived in corporate America, consultants were pushing many different problem-solving methods, sure that each one was one size fits all. I remember traveling with senior executives who had no practical experience in operational excellence. They walked through the airport and picked up a book about Six Sigma black belts. The new mandate: every plant needed to train managers to be Six Sigma black belts. The same executives read *The Toyota Way* and insisted that we do 10 Kaizen events. They weren't truly interested in actually pursuing continuous improvement, but they did enjoy the illusion.

Companies easily get caught up in management fads. Goodyear is no different. We used Six Sigma as well as A3, a structured problem solving and continuous improvement approach that was first employed at Toyota. Sometimes we wasted time considering whether we preferred orange- or tangerine-flavored management systems.

At the root, all of these methods have something in common: They're all based on a version of "plan, do, check, adjust." They all include a variation of "prove it, trust it, challenge it, and replicate it." There is no single "right" choice of a management system, any more than there is a single correct choice of spouse or profession. The right choice is the one that your company can commit to. Flitting from one option to another won't get you where you want to go.

Building a culture of continuous improvement, on the other hand, is the winning ticket. Create a culture where "plan, do, check, and adjust," as well as "prove it, trust it, challenge it, and replicate it," done over and over again, are normal operating procedure. That's the goal beyond the tools of operational excellence. Embed those attitudes in your organization and it will succeed.

> There is no single "right" choice of a management system, any more than there is a single correct choice of spouse or profession. The right choice is the one that your company can commit to implementing.

A winning organization also has a leader who works to earn people's respect. Being liked is nice. Being respected is mission critical, and it starts with respecting other people. Notice them. Listen to them. Good leaders measure what matters, but great leaders embrace the fact that not everything that matters can be measured.

I coached my son in basketball, and he made the team that he wanted to be part of. But the coaching wasn't the only thing that got him there. The time and attention from me, his father, was at least as important as anything I ever told him about basketball.

Every day that the Goodyear plant in Fayetteville made 38,000 tires, we celebrated. Eventually we were able to make 40,000 tires a day, because our efficiency had improved that much. As the plant's leader, I went out and got the orders for that extra capacity, competing with other Goodyear plants for the work. In addition to job security and a profit-sharing plan, I paid our associates in respect, trust, and value.

The Fayetteville plant has empowered and engaged our associates to choose the path of improvement. We built trust and communicated in ways that provided improved bottom-line results in weeks not years. Our team drove plant output from 31,000 tires per day to 38,000 in six months by strategically linking the organization to build trust through all layers, including floor operators; using straightforward deliberate clarity at a person-to-person level; and rewarding and recognizing individual contributions. We achieved a 23 percent productivity improvement by making 7,000 more tires per day with the same time and money. That gave the bottom line an additional $210,000 every day.

As evidence that these improvements were true productivity increases, our cost per unit dropped by more than 10 percent in the same time period.

For us, the game changers were:

- Defining winning by deploying strategy at all levels,
- Aligning to win by practicing extreme ownership at all levels, and
- Executing winning by managing the intersections.

These practices created our incredible results. They can help your company, too.

CONSIDER THIS

As you complete this chapter, consider:

- How can scientific thinking and deliberate practice improve your organization's results?
- What metrics tell you whether your company is winning or losing?
- If you could ask your employees anything, what would you like to know?
- How effective is your continuous improvement process?
- Do you recognize people for following the process?

CHAPTER 7

Governance

We've talked about the first three parts of winning: defining your purpose and goals, developing and deploying a strategy to reach those goals, and executing your strategy through every level and person in your organization. We also demonstrated how to build a continuous improvement culture. With those elements in place, it's time to discuss the next aspect of your plan: governance.

Governance is the glue of operational excellence, the consistent practices that keep a company executing its strategies and continuously improving. Strategies are a bit like physical therapy. Tell a physical therapist that "it hurts when I do this," and the therapist can generally devise stretches and strengthening exercises that let you move without pain. But stop doing those exercises and you're very likely to end up back where you started. Governance practices help an organization stick with a plan.

You've worked hard to put key performance indicators and actions in place. Good governance helps make them automatic, a part of your organization's culture that no one needs to think about. At some point in the distant past, someone probably taught you to brush your teeth before going to bed. First this person brushed your teeth for you, and then she taught you to do it yourself, every night without fail. You saw your parents and siblings brushing their teeth before bed, too. Now you always brush your teeth at bedtime. You never wonder if you should clean your teeth this evening. You just do it; so does everyone else.

But though people have been cleaning their teeth for centuries, regular toothbrushing only came into vogue in Europe in the late 1800s. Some Americans took up the habit, but daily brushing didn't become a cultural norm in the United States until after the second world war, when returning soldiers kept up the habit they'd formed in the military.

Think about that for a moment. Someone in the US military decided that service members should brush their teeth every day as part of overall personal hygiene.

> **A company's winning streak should outlast the leader who initially championed it.**

That person did such a thorough job of instilling that requirement that it became an unquestioned part of every day. When war ended and soldiers, sailors, and pilots could go home again, they happily stopped wearing their uniforms, sleeping in foxholes, and eating military rations. But they didn't stop brushing their teeth. They kept it up and taught the habit to their families, with such success that the global oral care market in 2019 was worth around $44.5 billion—all because someone thought the military would be healthier if its members cleaned their teeth.

That's the degree of cultural acceptance and embedding a practice you're aiming toward. You want your standards and system of continuous improvement to become an integral part of your organization.

You also want a system that will survive your departure. A company's winning streak should outlast the leader who initially championed it. Governance should help strategy, alignment, and execution become embedded in an organization's cultural life, so that when leadership inevitably changes, the organization still adheres to its winning systems and processes.

HARD ON THE PROCESS, EASY ON THE PEOPLE

A servant leadership model in which executives give workers the tools they need and let them take the lead in creating the process works well. But that alone does not create evangelism. To engrain processes, leaders must be hard on the process, so they can be easy on the people. Creating any working standard or specification should be a deliberate act. Notice a potential improvement, plan the improvement, and execute the idea. Then go back and check. Did the new procedure actually make things better in a material way? If so, implement that improvement everywhere you can.

Throughout your organization, workers should be executing tasks using efficient methods, every time they do that task. People don't show up and do their jobs using whatever means come to mind that day according to the moods they're in. There's a procedure, a recipe, for every job you do. If we think we can improve on the procedure, we plan (define), document (measure), evaluate (analyze), implement (improve), and standardize work (control). We plan the improvement. We prove it, challenge it, trust it and replicate it across common machine platforms and processes. Is the change a good one? Could it be better?

I saw this when I moved to the Goodyear plant in Lawton, Oklahoma. Lawton was the flagship Goodyear factory, and it was doing well, with 3,000 people making nearly 65,000 tires a day. I didn't need to rescue the plant. My challenge there was to take the operation from good to great. The plant had robust processes that outlasted plant managers, who changed over every two years. The foundation of consistency was the leadership team, who were relentless as they developed the operating and management processes. Personally, though, they treated workers gently. If the specifications said add crude rubber in step 1, synthetic rubber in step 2, and carbon black in step 3, it was a sin to violate the sequence. When operators followed the specifications and delivered good performance, they were applauded and recognized for following the process and getting good results.

At the same time that we celebrated workers for following the process, we constantly worked to simplify and standardize work procedures. Management constantly reviewed operations for compliance to the standards. You can't do this work from an office. It's vitally important to get out on the work floor and observe what's actually going on.

I watched machine changeovers in Lawton and noticed that we were not following the process. Change times were all over the place, from 20 minutes to two hours. Leaders let workers circumvent the changeover process, which specified that change material should be held in the designated prestaging area. Equipment wasn't staged to be ready for the workers, and people weren't notified about the coming changeover. Operators had created the standard process for machine changeovers, but they weren't following it. When we held people to the standard in Lawton, we cut changeover time by half.

All over the Lawton plant, we eliminated MUD—miscellaneous unidentified down time—and converted it to productivity. By being hard on the process, we minimized wasted motion and schedules that involved waiting. Lawton had scheduled performance peaks, making 65,000 tires one day every month on an occasion they called Big Dog Day. I wanted Big Dog Month, when we would consistently make 65,000 tires every day. To do that, we had to be hard on the process. This gave us the highest probability of achieving the best results. By constantly looking for ways to improve our processes and then committing to following the processes, we began making 65,000 tires every day at the same costs, specifications, and standards.

Humans make habits for all kinds of funny reasons. When the usual way we do things isn't the best way to do things, we can replace old routines with new habits based on evidence. We can incorporate these new procedures and methods into the standard process by following the prove it, challenge it, trust it, replicate it process.

Think about successful franchises. McDonald's is a good example of being hard on the process. You may not think theirs are the best hamburgers, but they might be the most consistent. Everything about every McDonald's restaurant is standardized, from the amount of time fries spend in hot oil to how workers wrap a cheeseburger. Because there is just one standard way to do every job, the functions are easy to learn and the business as a whole is almost infinitely scalable.

In addition to serving as a source of more and better ideas, creating a culture that accepts and celebrates every good idea will make your life and those of your managers much easier. Your employees own specific jobs. Letting them really oversee those areas means that you don't have to. I remember a senior vice president who came to Goodyear from ConAgra Foods. He said, "I look at management systems at ConAgra, and it's all about command and control. It created an environment where we were all managing two levels lower than we should have been managing."

There's been an evolution, not just of the workforce, but also of accountability in ownership, and it reflects the difference that vice president from ConAgra saw between the two companies. The old days saw autocratic leadership. Today's environment has people owning their jobs, leading from a position where they're treated like adults, have the autonomy to do their jobs, and be the CEOs of their own work.

In letting go of micromanagement, however, you are loosening the reins, not riding an untrained or undirected horse. Everyone in the organization is accountable to daily management meetings. These are not just a place to tell a manager what's wrong, although that's part of their purpose. They are also a point of contact where workers tell managers what they need in order to do their best work.

You've noticed that the Wi-Fi is out, and you need Wi-Fi to do your work? The daily management meeting is your opportunity to tell me about the problem. Then it's my job to make sure that we fix the Wi-Fi. You've noticed that your workspace could be more efficient if the doors had lever knobs instead of round knobs? Make a good case for the change, and I'll see that you get the lever knobs. Don't just tell me what's wrong. Be intentional in suggesting a solution.

WHAT YOU ACCEPT IS THE STANDARD

Create a standard and hold fast, because what you accept, you cannot change. The minute you walk past a broken window or a puddle on the floor without taking corrective action, that broken window or puddle becomes the standard, no matter what the rulebook says. We get what we tolerate.

This is true of both leadership and behavioral standards. Leadership standards are a guide for actions that govern group structure in a specific environment. Leaders need standards for both organizational behavior and performance. As we saw in the previous section, when a company pursues excellent, leadership standards have a lot to do with shaping its culture into one that solves problems and drives performance.

Larry Robbins, my first boss and mentor at Goodyear, took me for a walk every day around Goodyear's plant in Freeport, Illinois, to look for people not following standards: violating run specs, not wearing PPE, quitting early, lining up at the time clock, taking long breaks. He looked for poor housekeeping, pointing out when tread traps were in the aisles and that created tripping hazards, roof leaks that created slipping hazards, tools lying on the floor, other items out of place, or people not using the correct tools and materials for a given job. He was teaching me how to lead in a way that instilled cultural norms, asking me, "Why do you accept that? If you walk past poor adherence to standards, it's a form of acceptance—and what you accept becomes the standard."

The president of Goodyear came to visit our plant while I worked for Larry. I was a frontline manager and production specialist at the time, and I had our team clean up for the president's visit. The place couldn't have looked any better if we had been in full dress military uniforms. Floors were swept, buffed, and shined. Tread storage traps were lined. I proudly showed Larry what we'd accomplished, and he smiled and said, "You got it, Taylor." I thought he meant that the president would like what he saw.

No, Larry said, I'd missed the point. He meant that I had finally raised my standard. The plant should be tour ready every day. Why would I clean up for the president, but not for myself or my team? Larry visited the shop floor every day. Why wasn't I cleaning up for him? Taking pride in small things cascades into taking pride in bigger things.

Behavioral standards shape culture because they influence people. Leaders who effectively lead change use some authority—we can hire and fire, after all—and a lot of influence. Effective leadership is less about your title and more about your values and actions. People follow leaders they trust and respect; both take a long time to earn and just a moment to lose.

> **Taking pride in small things cascades into taking pride in bigger things.**

A leader's core function is to set the tone for success by both stating and modeling clear expectations. That's the foundation of a high-performance organizational culture and the way leaders can drive continuous improvement culture while also growing in confidence as leaders.

Before you can set behavioral standards for other people, though, you need to set some for yourself. Like a rock star, leaders are always onstage, even when they're backstage or back at the hotel. A leader's attitude is just as important as strategy in driving organizational success. What you do and how you behave shapes your team's overall disposition and culture. Just as the Rolling Stones take their cues from Mick Jagger, your team looks to you.

> **Effective leadership is less about your title and more about your values and actions.**

Model the behavior you want to see from your employees. You should assess your actions from their point of view. Are you holding yourself to the same standards? Do you have an internal continuous improvement mindset, striving to do everything a little better from one day to the next? Do you accept and learn from mistakes? Are you humble, vulnerable, and uncompromising? Do you have a healthy balance of confidence, ownership, and openness? Are the people around you able to see that you have high expectations for yourself?

Expecting more from your people than you do from yourself is a recipe for trouble. As anyone who has ever had (or been) a child can tell you, followers have an uncanny ability to sniff out hypocrisy in leaders. People will do as you do, not as you say, so make certain that your actions line up with what you hope to see from the other people in your organization. You are their role model. If you trash hotel rooms, they will take that as implicit permission to start tossing lamps.

That's not to say that you need to be a saint to earn other people's trust and respect. You do need to stand up for what's right, even (and perhaps especially) when what's right is not convenient. In North Carolina, the Goodyear plant I ran had a profit-sharing plan in which workers got a bonus when we met our goals. A mathematical error meant that the bonus wasn't paid out when it should have been, and other administrators suggested that we simply ignore that bonus and pay out the next one on time. Going back to the relevant paperwork would otherwise have been a hassle. I objected and insisted on doing the right thing; the company paid out the bonus, and the union president and I were able to announce the bonus together.

You don't need to have all the answers, either. Everyone needs a coach from time to time. When you find yourself unsure of what to do, you can ask for help and guidance. Develop mentors, friends, and colleagues who share common values and standards who are willing to give you reality checks and advice when you need them. You can return the favor when they need a helping hand.

DO YOU GET WHAT YOU EXPECT, OR EXPECT WHAT YOU GET? "PROTECT HOME PLATE"

Your standards for yourself ripple outward to help create your standards for the organization. Standards can change over time, as circumstances evolve. But once you've decided on appropriate standards and put them in place, you should not compromise them. Hold to your expectations and standards.

Sometimes it's tempting to adjust standards. Maybe a leader particularly likes someone who isn't meeting the standard, or it feels like too much work to enforce a standard on top of everything else you do in a day. But once set, those standards are not negotiable, and it is part of your job to stand behind them. (It should go without saying that adjusting a standard so you can punish someone you dislike is completely unacceptable. I find that, when leaders are tempted to adjust standards, it is typically out of fatigue or a desire to cut a likeable person a break.)

I sometimes make presentations with a home plate hung around my neck. My point is that no matter who you are, how well you play, or how much the coach likes you, home plate is 17 inches across (Figure 7.1). You're in Little League? Home plate is 17 inches across. You're in the World Series? Home plate is still 17 inches across. It doesn't get wider based on how badly you want to pitch a fair ball. (I got this idea from college baseball coach John Scolinos.)

FIGURE 7.1 Home Plate

Leaders can find sticking to standards very painful, especially when someone they care about isn't meeting them. When I was a running back in eighth grade, my football team was the best high school team in Texas. With an average of six touchdowns per game, I was important to its performance. My mother said that I could play as long as my grades were at least B's.

Just before a big game, I got a report card that contained six A's and one F. She told me that I wasn't playing in that important game. I was very upset. The school principal, athletic director, and team coach visited my mother. She said, "If you're here to talk about raising that F to at least a B, you're welcome to stay. But if you are here to talk about football, then I will have to ask you to leave. The standard is the standard." Our team lost the game, 54 to zero.

On her deathbed, my mother told me that she had anguished over that decision. She made up her mind when she realized that education was the way forward for me, and that I would have to hold other people to standards as a future leader. "I'm so proud that I held you to the standard," she told me, "because it helped shape you into the leader and person you are today."

In practice, you won't treat everyone the same way, because the people in your organization all have different needs. But you should treat everyone fairly. That includes being open to feedback from everyone, no matter what jobs they hold or how well they perform their duties.

Remember that ego erodes effectiveness. Guidelines need to be reasonable and clearly connected to your organization's purpose and goals. Don't attempt to adjudicate what color socks your people wear if sock color has nothing to do with the reasons that your company exists. Employees need and deserve to make independent decisions about the things that don't legitimately affect their jobs.

You want your enterprise to own its norms, not to make norms dependent solely on a leader's whims. You might have more authority than any one of your workers, but taken together, those workers outnumber you. You can't order culture change and expect it to happen. People need to buy in to what you're doing, especially since you can't always be around.

> **Remember that ego erodes effectiveness.**

At the very least, you should have high standards around safety, quality, and housekeeping.

Safety Is the Greatest Value Leaders Can Offer Their People

No job is worth injury or death, and strong safety standards can prevent catastrophe from happening. "Lucky" doesn't really count in manufacturing; if you violate a safety standard, a machine can kill you. As a leader, you let your team down in a profound way when you don't enforce safety standards.

At one of the Goodyear plants I managed, new hires often got hurt. One problem was that they didn't stand out as the people who were still learning how to stay safe. We bought them shirts in bright fluorescent colors and had them wear those shirts while they were in training to remind everyone that these people needed to take special care. Once they were certified on their machines, they got the official Goodyear racing jacket.

Organizations that have poor safety performance tend not to enforce rules around safety. The official rules say that workers have to wear personal protective equipment (PPE), such as hard hats and gloves, to keep them from being severely hurt or killed. In most cases, a manufacturing factory is not a physically gentle place. Ignoring safety standards can be fatal. I've seen workers fall down manholes or crushed by machinery—all preventable if people just follow the safety policies.

Managers who routinely walk past people who are not wearing PPE, without comment, make it acceptable for employees to ignore safety procedures. Early in my career, when I was a third-shift supervisor, I actually caught employees having sex in a snowplow truck while the truck was stored in a shed. It felt like a free-for-all. There was a rulebook somewhere, but it was clear that it was gathering dust. In practice, the plant accepted a lack of ownership, the regular breaking of rules, and all kinds of problematic behavior.

As a plant manager, I demanded that people wear PPE. When I saw managers quietly walk past employees who lacked the appropriate gear, I walked over and asked those employees nicely, "Mr. Smith, please wear your PPE. This is for your safety." Then I asked Mr. Smith's manager to come over and said, "Mr. Smith isn't wearing his PPE. Could you please make sure that Mr. Smith wears his PPE?" I also made sure that Mr. Smith had everything he needed and that his protective equipment was a good fit, because you can't safely operate machinery while wearing gloves that are too big.

If I found the supervisor again ignoring Mr. Smith's failure to wear his PPE, I gave that supervisor a three-day suspension from work, because he wasn't doing his job of holding his workers to the standard. Mr. Smith also got three days at home without pay, because he didn't hold himself to the standard. The word went through the plant: Billy Taylor isn't kidding. The safety standards are nonnegotiable. Standards around quality and housekeeping are only a whisker less important.

Build Quality and It Will Build You

Ignoring quality standards will eventually put your organization out of business. In particular, you should set a high standard for rewarding value created, not time spent.

Yes, people are expected to be at their jobs during work hours, and you will still want to consider their loyalty, dedication, and sense of service to the organization. But if you put a premium on actions that create value, then your people will be much more likely to perform those actions. Reward individuals and teams for the value they create. At Goodyear it was unacceptable to pass on poor quality components, such as tread, to upstream tire assembly. We empowered operators to shut down equipment to resolve unsafe conditions or correct quality issues. We reinforced the importance of value by recognizing workers for preventing or catching substandard products. When employees caught their own mistakes, such as a wrong setup, we didn't discipline them. We documented what had happened so we could avoid the problem in the future, but there were only positive consequences for workers. We made it safe to point out problems.

Housekeeping Is Critical to Both Safety and Quality

Whether it's getting paperwork done on time or keeping workspaces tidy, housekeeping is a crucial component of both safety and quality.

I spent perhaps 80 percent of my time walking around the factory floor. At one point, I saw a worker sitting at his bench, reading a magazine. He made no attempt to hide the magazine, get back to work, or look busier when he saw me. He glanced up, saw me, and went back to his article. His workspace was a mess.

"Sir," I said to him, "I need your help to start turning this plant around. Your workspace is a mess. What would you need to make it clean and tidy?" Well, he replied, he'd need a bucket and some cleaning supplies. I put together everything he'd listed and brought it over to him.

The next time I saw his work area, the difference was remarkable. Tools were neatly organized. Surfaces gleamed. "Wow!" I exclaimed. "Your area looks fantastic. Do you think you could present your workspace to other employees and explain how you got your result?" Justifiably proud of his work, the man did just what I'd asked, showing off his area and discussing his methods with his peers.

My method here was deliberate. I approached him as the expert on what he needed to do a better job. I brought him the resources he asked for. I celebrated his excellent result and asked him to teach other people how to do what he had done.

The less visible results were even more important. My exchange with this man built his ownership of his work area. I could have just been another boss, stopping by to give another order. Instead, treating him as an expert and a teacher meant that he took ownership of his workspace and how it was organized. Celebrating his success turned him into an evangelist. He became a role model.

THE TRUST FACTOR

To many people, "lean management" sounds as though it will involve cutting jobs and costs, not workplace improvement. I was able to succeed in both union and nonunion factories because I specifically told everyone—workers, shop stewards, and union brass—that jobs would get better, not go away.

Instead of making cuts, I met with workers on all three shifts to explain that I would use lean management principles to enhance workforce capability and value. The changes also made jobs much more interesting. Following an autocrat's instructions to the letter, never getting to make an alteration or follow your own best judgment—that isn't an especially rewarding way to spend 40 hours a week. Jobs that let workers use their brains and innovate are much more satisfying. In the end, we ended up hiring more workers, and we saved money by developing a tire that we could produce for half the cost of what was already on the market.

I also invited union officials to every meeting I held. I had standards for every meeting attendee, such as a strict "no swearing" rule. I had to reinforce that standard once by asking a union president to leave until he could follow that guideline. Overall, however, that blanket invitation helped me establish transparency. I wasn't there to say one thing and do another. I demonstrated my own standards for integrity. People became willing to trust me and to follow those standards by exhibiting their own integrity.

When they saw that I meant what I said, unions and their members became my evangelists, helping my strategy go viral at the factory. When Goodyear ultimately closed the plant in Tyler, workers went from there to other Goodyear factories all across the country. When I visited a plant in Alabama where many former Tyler workers had found jobs, people wanted to take a break from their machines so they could say hi to me. People are people, union or not.

In truth, I did fire a few people, but not because I was trying to reduce overall head count. Some workers weren't in the right jobs, and I worked with those people to find the right places to showcase their talents.

> To inspire trust, when you say what you will do, you must do what you say.

Unfortunately, other workers simply weren't willing to meet my standards. I say "willing," because I've found that while you can coach ability, you can't coach desire. It is also a challenge to coach basic ethics, which is why I have fired employees who have lied to me.

In Fayetteville, my second-in-command thought there should be different standards for him. A Saturday morning meeting was his idea, and he scheduled his team to attend that meeting—but he never showed up. He should have worked one weekend a month, but he somehow didn't turn up for those shifts, either. I explained the standard to him. I was at the next Saturday morning meeting, but he was at a Vanderbilt University football game. He understood what I expected and chose not to meet that expectation. The way I see it, he essentially fired himself. You have a right to fail as an individual, but you do not have the right to abandon the playbook and make decisions that cause the team to fail—not without consequences. To inspire trust, when you say what you will do, you must do what you say.

CONSEQUENCES OF POOR LEADERSHIP

Leaders are operating under a microscope today, with social media amplifying the results of everything they do. News of a leader's actions and inactions has always made its way around a community, but social media means that people now hear the news much faster. As a result, every encounter matters. It's ever more important to understand that low standards—or failing to uphold high standards—can have a potentially irreversible negative effect on leaders' credibility and their company's success.

Leaders who have low standards will also have difficulty inspiring confidence, which is crucial for organizational buy-in. People are naturally drawn to strong leaders, and the weak leader gives up this advantage. Weak leaders will also have trouble building organizational alignment, because organization members will be slow to throw in their lot with the people they find inconsistent, indecisive, or less than credible.

Leaders who can't make up their minds may also sow divisions and misunderstandings within the group. The inability to trust a leader means that people will be slow to adopt the process or grant the leader the cultural right to change. The organization may have difficulty attracting and retaining top talent.

Failure to show leadership by holding to standards can seriously affect employee morale and even damage a company's bottom line. Weak leadership leads to low employee retention—most folks don't want to work in a place where intoxicated people drive forklifts if they have other choices—and this demotivates the remaining employees. Why work hard if it's perfectly acceptable to hardly work?

Because the environment isn't one where the best employees would choose to work, the organization will have trouble attracting and retaining talent. People naturally want to find purpose and provide value in their jobs, because rallying around a purpose helps them feel a sense of pride and belonging. Value gives them a sense of their impact on results. Leaders with high standards shine a light on individual and team contributions, which the best employees find attractive and nearly everyone finds inspiring. Positive recognition encourages workers to up their game.

REGULAR ALIGNMENT MEETINGS KEEP AN ORGANIZATION ON TRACK

Strong leadership and high standards are also reflected in regular alignment meetings, which are an important part of keeping any large organization rowing in a single direction, and of addressing issues when they come up.

At the Goodyear plants I managed, we had five tiers of employees: C-level executives (level 5), plant managers (level 4), department managers (level 3), area supervisors (level 2), and hourly workers (level 1). Each intersection between the tiers had regular huddles, which looked like this:

- Area supervisors (level 2) check in with hourly workers (level 1) every day, often more than once and sometimes even hourly.

- Department managers (level 3) huddle with area supervisors (level 2) every day.
- Plant managers (level 4) talk with department managers (level 3) every week.
- C-suite executives (level 5) talk with plant managers (level 4) every month.

Every one of these conversations is a reality check. Are we following the plan, doing what we said we would do? Do we have everything we need to do our jobs effectively? Are we following our standards for PPE, quality, and housekeeping? Are we removing barriers and constraints to our plan and our standards? If we have problems with materials, personnel, machines, or anything else, are we solving those problems?

Very often, it's possible to solve problems within the regular tiered meetings. When that doesn't happen, problems bubble upward until they reach a tier where someone does have the ability to resolve the issues. Maybe the hourly workers in charge of the bathrooms have worn-out mops. Either the hourly supervisor orders new mops, if that's part of her job, or she talks to the department manager, who can then buy the necessary supplies.

Lean management does include regular performance reviews. At every review, I focus on one question: Are you working the process that you're meant to be working? What were you hired to do? What are your roles and responsibilities? I use the meeting as a time to revisit standards and expectations.

REAL RECOGNITION—
WEEKLY MEETINGS SHOW OFF
WORKER-LED IMPROVEMENTS

In addition to our tiered meetings, the plants I ran also had weekly gatherings where hourly workers could present their continuous improvement projects on the shop floor, showing off process improvements when they had found better ways to do their jobs. Sometimes they volunteered their discoveries. Other times I or another manager informally caught them doing something well on one of our many walk-arounds.

Before I look for things that are going wrong and need to change, I look for things that people are already doing well. People want to be seen and recognized for what they're doing right. Leaders make a mistake when they focus immediately on what's wrong. It keeps the leader's ego front and center, which isn't a good thing. To get buy-in, you should build on what is already working in a culture, putting your people front and center. Remove the things that deteriorate that good culture. It's a little like the old adage: in order to sculpt an angel, get a block of marble and remove everything that isn't an angel.

In addition to offering the opportunity to be recognized for doing something inventively and well, these weekly meetings also reinforce the value of following the process into a continuous improvement cycle. When we have a standard, we prove it, trust it, challenge it, and replicate it. The standard changes when someone shows us a way to do things that's demonstrably better. We celebrate people who do that.

TRUST AND VERIFY

Bingo audits are the second way I catch people doing things well. Maybe there are 30 machines. Each machine gets a number, and you draw one of those numbers at random. The leadership team walks to that number's machine and makes sure that everything with that machine and its operator is as it should be: PPE, an up-to-date visual management system, in possession of everything the worker needs to do the job, operator adherence to processes, following quality and client specifications, using proper tools. (Fort Bragg, where I've given talks about operational excellence, uses this system.)

These spot checks accomplish three things. First and most obviously, they keep people on their toes. Everyone is eligible for a bingo audit, so everyone needs to consistently meet the standards to pass one.

The standards, however, are about helping. They aren't punitive. If someone isn't meeting those standards, I want to help that person by getting her the tools she needs or solving whatever work problems she has. A bingo audit is a place to solve problems on the spot, without waiting for those difficulties to bubble through layers of management. It's not about criticism, but rather about professional transparency.

Second, bingo audits provide another opportunity to push the wheel of continuous improvement. If I haven't heard directly from a worker who has found a better way to do something and I haven't seen that improvement in action as I walk around the shop floor, there's still a good chance that I'll find out about it during a bingo audit.

That invention could become the new standard if the worker is willing to go through the process of proving and challenging it with other people in the organization.

Third, bingo audits are an opportunity to praise, connect, and build relationships with people you might not otherwise interact with regularly. I use these interactions to let people know how valued they are. Not everything that matters can be measured, and I like to remind workers of that when I can.

Take care to praise people for working the process, and not for going off script in a way that doesn't involve continuous improvement. You don't want people to get so much positive feedback for putting out fires that they become arsonists. You want your people to become fire prevention experts.

CONTINUOUS LEARNING FOR LEADERS

Everyone needs a coach. We've talked a lot in this book about how to manage an organization's work processes so the company can win. But managing winning is a job, too. As with the other tasks in your company, it's helpful to learn from other people as you refine your approach to leading positive change.

I recall a meeting that I thought would end in a promotion and pay raise. Instead my boss had written me up. He said my standards were too low. That night, my boss and I went out for a drink to talk about standards, expectations, winning, and the connections between these things. "What do you need from me in order to deliver on my expectations?" he asked me. On reflection, there wasn't anything I needed from him. What I needed was to have a more concrete definition of winning, and to communicate that definition to my team. My operators and service people weren't aware of our losses or how their behavior affected the plant.

I was too quick to accept behavior that clearly violated standards, too. Operators were running codes out of sequence because that was more convenient for them. Setup technicians each had their own processes for setting up tread runs. Workers weren't following the quality department's recipes or line-run speeds, which meant that lots of work had to be redone. We were losing an average of between 2,000 and 4,000 minutes every month to tasks that had to be redone. When we began following the processes and standards, we lost just 15 minutes that month.

The boss celebrated the process and praised us for following it. We had a cookout. The company newsletter wrote about how the team improved by adhering to the process. Our stellar performance continued. Two months later, the boss called me back to his office, smiled, and gave me my long-awaited promotion.

I learned another lesson when MidMichigan Health CEO Diane Postler-Slattery invited me to speak at her organization's annual operating meeting. She asked me to wear all pink: a pink suit, a pink tie, a pink shirt, and even pink socks, if I had some. What an odd request, I thought to myself. Still, I complied with her request. When I showed up in my pink outfit, Diane greeted me at the door. She was in a princess costume.

My keynote speech went well. After thanking me, Diane said, "Okay, Billy, let's dance to close this meeting." Silentó's song "Watch Me (Whip/Nae Nae)" came on over the speakers, and Diane and I—both over age 50—started doing the whip and the nae nae. A few seconds later, our professionally attired audience leaped to their feet and joined us.

Diane had created an environment where it was safe to be a little silly. It was safe to try something new. That went a long way to explaining why everyone was engaged and felt empowered, as well as why her team's innovations put them well ahead of the competition. Diane's team was so successful because she created a place that embraced creative disruption. That fed her continuous improvement culture.

The experience opened my eyes to a new possibility: engaging my people to move beyond fear. (Beyond the fear of trying new things, that is. I still wanted them to have a healthy fear of what might happen if they didn't wear their PPE.) I realized that psychological safety is as important as physical safety and began consciously working to improve psychological safety throughout my career.

REALITY AND REFLECTION

Visual management boards are an invaluable way to figure out what's going well, what's going wrong, and where. We also used an additional method for finding out what was right and wrong; we asked our workforce.

We did this in the context of an activity called the mirror exercise, so called because it helps an organization see its true reflection. We invited workers into a room filled with tables that each displayed a large board where questions were posted about a particular aspect of work. Sticky notes and pens were nearby. We invited workers to answer our questions anonymously, by writing their thoughts on the sticky notes and posting those notes on the board.

For example, safety was an area where we wanted to ask questions. The safety board queries included:

- Is your business center leadership concerned about keeping you safe?
- Do you think people in this area knowingly act unsafely by not following existing rules?
- Do you think workers in this area take safety seriously?
- What does your business center do right around safety?
- What else can we do to help improve safety?
- On a scale of 1 to 5, how much are *you* in control of safety?

We were also interested in workers' thoughts about product quality. Our questions on this subject included:

- When was product quality best in this plant? What did it look like?
- On your job, what do you do to improve quality or reduce waste?
- If you are working on machines, what are the top three scrap issues on your machine?
- How do you know that you had a good day on waste/scrap performance?
- Are you able to make a changeover or a start-up without making rework or scrap? What prevents

    you from making a changeover without rework
    or scrap?
- Do you get the opportunity to work on
improving quality? If yes, what do you get to do?

We then collected the answers and decided what we could realistically work to improve or address. Some fact-finding was often necessary to make sure that the situation was as the employee described. Though we had to throw out a few comments, workers were overall constructive and accurate in what they had to say.

We chose the issues that we would address and decided what strategies we would use, at least initially, and made that information and the ultimate results public for everyone in the plant. People felt heard, which is vitally important, and management got inside information and opportunities to fix problems, remove constraints, and otherwise improve the operation that we might not otherwise have had.

WORKING FOR THE PEOPLE YOU LEAD

Any manager worth her salt will consider what factors might help her workers perform better. In my experience with companies large and small, the key to success is leadership commitment. As a leader, I work for my team. It's my job to eliminate barriers to their success.

Just about any work area could probably be improved in ways that make employees' lives easier and therefore more productive. Leaders must empower the people doing the work.

This book is all about making changes that improve performance. That's what lean operations do. By going through our days with the expectation that improvement is possible, we prime ourselves to notice places and instances where change can make a positive difference.

When I started at Goodyear in Tyler, I faced a plant full of workers who didn't know me from Adam and had no desire to let me change anything about their working conditions. They saw me as an agent of risk, rather than an agent of opportunity. In their minds, any plans I might have were mine alone.

Every job is a series of actions. Company performance improves because individuals practice the key performance actions that cumulatively move the measurements, or key performance indicators. When we break down a job into discreet actions, it's much easier for the person doing the job to identify actions that will improve the metrics.

When you do a job and identify ways that you can do it better, share that information with your peers, as you are an owner. Recall the employee with the messy workspace? Our interaction turned one employee into the CEO of his workbench. Because he also became the local clean-space guru, he could help other workers become the CEOs of their own workspaces. He wasn't grudgingly, half-heartedly going through the motions because a boss told him he had to. He was powerful. He had the tools and ideas he needed to change.

Every person in the factory needs a similar level of ownership and investment in their job. It wasn't enough for me to care about the plant's performance, or for other managers to be invested. Winning requires an entire plant full of CEOs.

CONNECTIONS, NOT COLLISIONS

In Fayetteville, we put management boards in a room called the Center of Excellence. It's the place where we post red/green indicators for safety, quality, delivery, and cost, as well as business units and product lines within the business units (Figure 7.2). If the indicators are green, all is well. When an indicator goes red, the management boards in the Center of Excellence tell us what's wrong and where. Sometimes we also need to investigate management boards at more granular levels, but the Center of Excellence always shows us where to dig to find the problem. In 10 seconds or less, you can find the constraints.

At one point, we hosted 10 high-school students for two weeks so they could learn how the core components of a linked operating system function for their senior capstone projects. They easily and intuitively understood the management boards. Their simplicity allows nearly anyone to walk in and see what's going on, just like a sports scoreboard.

Figures 7.3 is the actual Center of Excellence used to lead and manage North America Commercial Operations. The top line indicates the functional targets, owners, and strategy. Below the functions, the model Links each plant's strategy, performance, and owners to the enterprise targets.

The design of the COE allows leadership to manage the intersections of functions and tiers, eliminating silos so that interactions are connections, not collisions. It's simple and easy to see where the issues are that constrain and bottleneck the organization. To prove the concept, we trained high school students as part of their

FIGURE 7.2 Management Board with Red/Green Indicators

181

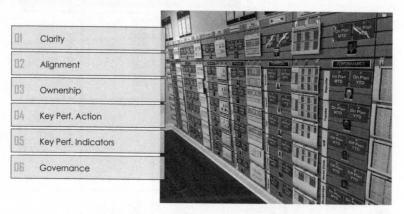

01	Clarity
02	Alignment
03	Ownership
04	Key Perf. Action
05	Key Perf. Indicators
06	Governance

FIGURE 7.3 Actual Center of Excellence

senior capstone project. At the end of two weeks, the students simulated a Monthly Operating Review with Senior Leaders to test the process for effectiveness. The students could pinpoint where the issues were that constrained the enterprise and they could also identify who owned what in the process. The president of the school and their parents were amazed at the student's business acumen accumulated through the process. Although they did not have the experience to resolve the issues, it was crystal clear that they knew what the issues were.

The Center of Excellence Center is also a place that fosters a culture of extreme ownership, enhances leadership development, drives best practice sharing, and effective problem-solving to drive and govern performance for enterprise sustainability.

CONSIDER THIS

As you finish this chapter, consider:

- How are you a positive model for your workforce? Are there ways in which you are not a positive model?
- What are your standards around safety, quality, and housekeeping?
- Does your organization tacitly accept lower standards than it should?
- Does your company have "recipes" for how it does things? How can you improve those procedures?
- List two ways that you can regularly try to catch your people doing things well.
- Are there other ways you can act as a servant leader by supporting the people who work for you?
- Why would the team follow you and your leadership team?

CONCLUSION

We've talked about defining winning, developing a winning plan, executing that plan, and governing the positive result, and about the vital importance of extreme clarity, engagement, empowerment, and ownership throughout your journey to winning.

The last point I want to make is that this system of operational excellence is scalable. I spent 12 years in Freeport, Illinois, in a variety of jobs: night shift floor supervisor, production specialist, and business center operations manager for component preparation, which involved running a third of the plant. I was plant manager in Kingman, Arizona, for two years and then spent time in Topeka, Kansas, as the business center manager for tire assembly and the finishing process. I managed Goodyear plants in Tyler, Texas; Lawton, Oklahoma; and Akron, Ohio. Then I ran Goodyear's North American commercial and off-highway operations. Before I left Goodyear, I also spent a year as the chief diversity and inclusion officer for Goodyear's global operations.

I developed and used the LinkedXL system through every job I had at Goodyear. Now I deploy it on behalf of my consulting clients. I've seen firsthand that this method is just about infinitely scalable. It creates a connected business model for any size or type of organization. You could use LinkedXL to run a corner shop or to run the North American operations of the world's third-largest tire manufacturer. It could help you run a household or run a global company.

I wish you the very best as you and your organization start winning too.

ACKNOWLEDGMENTS

I am extending my heartfelt thanks to my wife Rachel, daughter Alexis, and son Alexander for their acceptance and patience during my entire career and the writing of my book. They are my greatest inspiration and the highlight of my life! My wife has endured a 30-plus year journey with Goodyear, through the research of the LinkedXL process, and writing of this book. She never complained, only greeted our challenges as a true partner and a "yes, we can do" attitude. She is my greatest support in life and business. Thanks for being my rock and best friend. Without my family, this book would not have become a reality. I love you.

I am extremely grateful to my parents Vera Taylor-Jones and Sheik Tehuti for their love, prayers, caring and sacrifices. I am very much thankful to my stepdad George Jones for his unwavering support. Also, I express my thanks to my brothers Everett, Derric, and Donnie Taylor. Allah Ray and Michael Richards, my sisters, sister-in-law and brother in laws, aunts and uncles, I am grateful for their support and valuable prayers.

I would like to express my deep and sincere gratitude to my LinkedXL Team, Dave Kutcher, Aaron Bushner, Joanna Mercado, Hannah Adams and Rachel for the support and the LinkedXL process rollout. Thanks to Teijin Automotive Technologies Executive Team of Chris Twining, COO and President; Steve Wisniewsk, CFO; Mike Bishop VP of Operations; Wayne Meyers VP of Quality and C.I.; and Jerry Reid Regional Ops. Director, for giving me the opportunity to conduct research and providing invaluable guidance throughout the impactful enterprise implementation. Thanks to Carey Noel, my Continuous Improvement Manager in Fayetteville. She was a groundbreaking Lean Practitioner, who was my Sensei. May you rest in peace.

I am grateful to have worked with the people, teams, and leaders in Goodyear Tire & Rubber Company. Plants: Freeport, IL, Kingman, AZ, Topeka KS, Tyler, Tx, Lawton, OK, Fayetteville, NC, Danville, VA – Statesville, NC, Stockbridge, GA, Social Circle, GA, and Innovation Center Manufacturing (ICM), OH. A 30-year career in North America Operations supporting the Consumer, Commercial, and Off-Highway businesses.

Thank you to my Goodyear friends and colleagues, Sammy Manored, "The General," Larry Robbins, Greg Guy, Chuck Grunder, Chris Werner, Pat Hurley, and Rich Kramer, CEO of Goodyear, for your leadership through-out my 30-year career. Larry and Greg, thank you for the opportunities, vision, sincerity, and motivation that have deeply inspired me. To The United Steel Workers of America, thanks for partnering with me to effectively "Change the Game" for American Manufacturing.

Thank you to The Shingo Institute and The Association of Manufacturing Excellence for reinforc-ing the lean and operational excellence methodology and proven practices to carry out the research and to present the research works as clearly as possible.

It was a great privilege and honor to work with Note Printing Australia. I am extremely grateful for what the organization has offered me in practical application of the Linked (Torque) process. Thanks to Doug Weintraub and The Bounce Innovation Hub team and Elijah Stambaugh. Thanks to the PPG Cleveland Team and Plant Manager Greg Kerr for your relentless pursuit of excellence and rolling out the LinkedXL process.

Special thanks to my publishing and content team. Judith Newlin, Senior Editor McGraw Hill; Scott Kurtz, Senior Editing Supervisor; Steve Straus; and Ingrid Case, my Content Architect, for the keen interest shown to complete this book from beginning to end successfully. Thanks to Susanne Schotanus and George Taninecz for being a source for guidance and giving me feedback. Thank you to Karen Martin, Founder and President of TKMG Academy and Author of *Clarity First* for inspiring me to write this book and connecting me with the right resources. My sincere gratitude to Richard Sheridan, CEO and cofounder of Menlo Innovations for the guidance and support.

I would like to say thanks to my friends from 4200 Burton, Fort Worth, Texas, Highland Hills, Dallas, Texas and friends from Prairie View A&M University, Omega Psi Phi Fraternity Inc, and Sigma Rhomeo for their constant encouragement. Thanks also to Ellis Jones, Gary Davis, and Billy O'Quinn for their genuine support throughout my career.

Finally, my thanks go to all the people who have supported me to complete the research work directly or indirectly in both large and small operations, corporations, and entrepreneurial companies, and for and not for profits organizations, that helped me prove the LinkedXL process works.

INDEX

Page numbers followed by *f* and *t* refer to figures and tables, respectively.

ABOUT THE AUTHOR

Billy Taylor is a leadership guru with more than 30 years of experience with The Goodyear Tire & Rubber Co. He served most recently as the head of North American commercial manufacturing and as chief diversity and inclusion officer. As the global head of diversity and inclusion for Goodyear, Taylor led diversity and inclusion strategies for 64,000 employees across the 22 countries where Goodyear operates. His work at Goodyear's plant in Lawton, Oklahoma, helped his team win the Shingo Prize Silver Medallion for Operational Excellence, an award that's considered the Nobel prize of operations.

He is currently the CEO of LinkedXL, a business operating systems architecting firm dedicated to implementing effective operating systems that drive sustainable results for client companies. Taylor has cemented a name for himself as an innovative and energetic industry professional with a passion for operational excellence. With deep industry knowledge, coupled with an analytical and detail-oriented, process-driven approach, Taylor has helped many high-profile companies, including Note Printing Australia, Teijin Automotive Technologies, and PPG Industries, build effective and sustainable operating systems.

A disciple of continuous improvement processes, Taylor's love for people inspires his commitment to helping others achieve their full potential. Taylor's servant-leadership abilities have earned him invitations to universities, international conferences, global publications, and the U.S. Army to demonstrate how to achieve and sustain effective results. Leveraging his business acumen and track record as a proven practitioner, Taylor's *The Winning Link* helps readers understand how to define, align, execute, and govern a winning operating system.

The National Diversity Council named Taylor as one of the Top 100 Diversity Officers in the United States in 2021. He has been featured among Oklahoma's Most Admired CEOs and is on the executive advisory board for the Shingo Institute and the Association of Manufacturing Excellence (AME), both leading organizations for operational excellence, business development, and cultural learning.

He earned a bachelor's degree in electrical engineering from Prairie View A&M University in Prairie View, Texas, and an MBA from Baker University in Baldwin City, Kansas.